The Complete Guide to
DECORATIVE
STAMPING

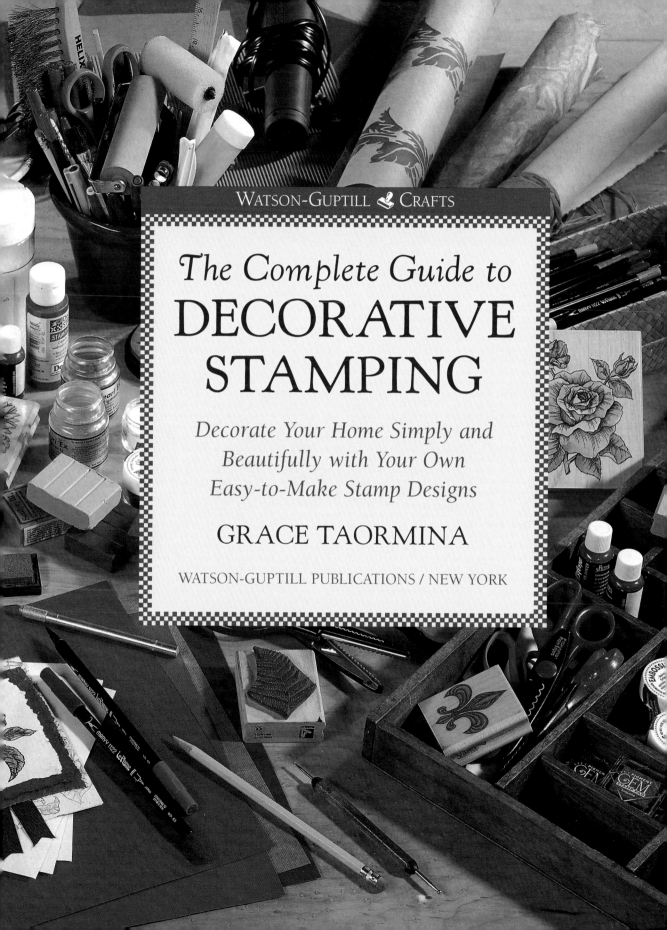

WATSON-GUPTILL ❦ CRAFTS

The Complete Guide to
DECORATIVE
STAMPING

*Decorate Your Home Simply and
Beautifully with Your Own
Easy-to-Make Stamp Designs*

GRACE TAORMINA

WATSON-GUPTILL PUBLICATIONS / NEW YORK

Senior Editor: Candace Raney
Edited by Joy Aquilino
Designed by Areta Buk
Graphic production by Ellen Greene

First published in 1998 by Watson-Guptill Publications,
a division of BPI Communications, Inc.,
1515 Broadway, New York, N.Y. 10036

Library of Congress Cataloging-in-Publication Data
Taormina, Grace.
    The complete guide to decorative stamping: decorate your home
simply and beautifully with your own easy-to-make stamp designs /
Grace Taormina.
        p.   cm.
    Includes index.
    ISBN 0-8230-0791-X
    1. Rubber stamp printing. 2. Interior decoration. I. Title.
TT867.T35   1998
761—dc21
                                                    98-12703
                                                    CIP

Manufactured in Italy

First printing, 1998

1 2 3 4 5 6 7 8 9 / 06 05 04 03 02 01 00 99 98

CONTRIBUTING DESIGNERS

The following designers contributed
stamping projects and techniques to
this book:

Lynn Damelio
Bunny plate *(page 54)*
Heat-transfer fish print shower curtain
(page 63)
Children's table and chairs *(page 87)*

Lea Everse
Stamped, hammered, and punched
metal accessories *(page 70)*

Dee Gruenig
Double-inked flower pots *(page 42)*

Kari Lee
Leather portfolio *(pages 150–154)*

Michelle Powell
Metal-trimmed mirror *(pages 146–149)*

Susan Pickering Rothamel
Mica collage table and matching lamp
(pages 92–95)

Erin Shetterly
Leaf-and-vine picture mat *(page 8)*
Puff paper and blind-embossed picture
(page 9)
Checkerboard heart box *(page 38)*
Fleur-de-lis collage mat *(pages 130–133)*

Deborah Tanaka
Pear pillow *(page 48)*
Gold-leaf-accented wooden box *(page 82,
lower right)*

Suze Weinberg
"Tiled" storage chest *(pages 96–99)*

Except as noted above, all projects
were designed by Grace Taormina.

PHOTOGRAPHERS
Sal Taormina
Allan Fine
David Belda

ILLUSTRATORS
Trish Heaney
Chris Errington
Donna Yuen

ACKNOWLEDGMENTS

This book is the culmination of the hard work and dedication of many special people. Without their talent, enthusiasm, and creativity, this book would not have been possible. I am truly blessed to have such a wonderful support system of intelligent and caring people in my life and I am deeply grateful to all of them. I would like to acknowledge the efforts of, and extend my deeply felt thanks to, the following individuals:

Lynn Damelio, who helped me coordinate all the details for this book and collect the supplies for the photographs, for her design and technical expertise, and for her seemingly unshakable composure (as our hand model she sat for hours on end).

Joann Miller, for her superb organizational skills in cataloging and proofreading, for her patience with me when changes were made, and, most of all, just for being a great sister.

Erin Shetterly, Clara Arriaga, and Susana Espinoza, for their help and talent in creating the step-by-step photographs, and for the extra responsibilities they shouldered in order to allow me to work on this book.

Sam and Tsoi Katzen and Kathleen O'Connell, for their complete faith in and support of this project, and for providing the resources and time to produce it.

At Watson-Guptill Publications, Candace Raney and Harriet Pierce, for asking me to do this book, and Joy Aquilino, for her wonderful support and talent as an editor.

Peter Fehler, for his expertise in working with wood, which allowed me to successfully complete some of the projects for this book.

Marjorie Pioli Interiors and Melody Celestino-Cretin, for loaning me furniture and accessories from their private collections.

Deborah Tanaka, for her artistic and technical skill.

Aida Simbe and Estela Celestino, for always helping out in a pinch.

My children, Joey and Rachel, for learning how to cook quick meals, and for enduring a household strewn with stamp supplies and projects.

Special thanks to my husband, Sal, for taking most of the photographs, and for his patience, love, and support.

Contents

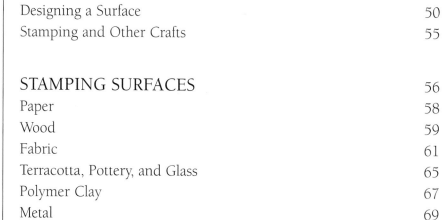

DECORATIVE STAMPING PROJECTS

Introduction

The creative boundaries of stamping have broadened considerably over the past few years. Novice and experienced stampers alike ingeniously seek out new materials, surfaces, and applications with which to express their artistry—a sure sign of this unusual craft's versatility. Once the exclusive domain of paper and rubber stamp enthusiasts, stamping has not only grown due to the variety of influences it has been exposed to (an inevitable consequence of its popularity), but it has also matured, giving rise to the development, reconsideration, and reinvention of a number of new creative options. The result: a craft that can be used to make elegant furniture, fabrics, and accessories, and that is also sophisticated enough to decorate an entire room.

By surveying stamping's sweeping landscape, from the basics to the latest in materials, surfaces, and styles, *The Complete Guide to Decorative Stamping* can help liberate the reader's creativity, allowing him or her to exploit the craft to its greatest potential. Although it is possible to follow all the instructions to the letter in order to reproduce the projects exactly as they are shown in the photographs, readers are encouraged to flex their creative muscles and devise their own original designs.

The first section, "Stamping Basics," reviews essential materials, from stamps (both commercially manufactured ready-mades and a range of surfaces that can be carved with original designs) to inks, paints, and key supplies, as well as some nice-to-have accessories. So that even a novice stamper can get started right away, the most basic of stamping techniques—inking a stamp, making a print, masking, embossing, and a few simple special effects—are also covered.

The leaf outlines and vines on this picture mat were hand drawn using brown and green paint markers.

"Color and Design" takes the mystery out of two inherently intimidating subjects, giving readers the tools they need to make informed and thoughtful decisions while still allowing them to acknowledge their own instincts and preferences. In addition, some ideas for combining stamping with other crafts are noted.

The investigative efforts of enthusiastic stampers, combined with some important technical advances in inks and paints, have made it possible to decorate an increasing number of surfaces with stamps. "Stamping Surfaces" examines the many choices available (and their technical requirements), including paper, wood, fabric, terracotta, glass, polymer clay, metal, and leather and suede.

The home is the most important place in a person's life. Because it's where we spend most of our time and should reflect who we are, it should be decorated to satisfy our own personal taste. "Stamped Interiors" makes this undertaking somewhat easier to cope with by providing an overview of the process of decorating a room with stamps, from evaluating its architectural features and furnishings to stamping its walls with an all-over pattern, a border, or a wreath.

In the final section, "Decorative Stamping Projects," four project categories—furniture, fabrics, interiors, and accessories—showcase a variety of designs and surfaces, as well as compatible crafting techniques and media. Use these projects to experiment with different motifs, color schemes, and techniques, allowing yourself to envision, then carry out, your own unique interpretations. Happy stamping!

Cast paper can be simulated by combining puff paint with blind embossing. In this example, rubber stamps were used as patterns for applying the puff paint, which was allowed to dry for 24 hours before heating to achieve a smooth finish.

STAMPING BASICS

The requirements for stamping are remarkably few: a stamp, some ink or paint, and a surface on which to make a print. By contrast, the number of choices available to fulfill each requirement can be overwhelming. For example, while commercially manufactured rubber and die-cut foam stamps can be easily obtained at a variety of retail outlets, stamp designs can also be cut from or carved out of sponges, potatoes, linoleum, printing blocks, erasers, and even "found" objects. This section also explains how to put these materials to use by covering some basic techniques, from making a print to creating special effects.

Stamp Fundamentals

In just the last few years, the craft of stamping has evolved to include an ever-increasing number of images, surfaces, and decorative effects. Its growing popularity has not only contributed to the extraordinary diversity of commercially produced stamps, but has inspired stampers to carve their own stamp images, as well as to experiment by printing with "found" objects.

A stamp image can generally be identified as either outline or broad-surface. An *outline stamp* is used to print the contour lines of an image, similar to a picture in a coloring book; any detailing is usually represented by stippling, shading, or cross-hatching. This type of image is usually stamped in a dark color, then colored in with markers, pencils, or paints if desired. In contrast, a *broad-surface stamp* uses a solid surface to print a bold image suggestive of a stencil print, generally eliminating the need for additional coloring.

Some of the earliest stamps were used to create patterns on textiles. These were typically intricate, abstract designs carved out of wood with sharp tools, similar in appearance to the woodblocks that present-day artists use to make prints. Many East Indian textiles are still printed with elaborately carved wood stamps.

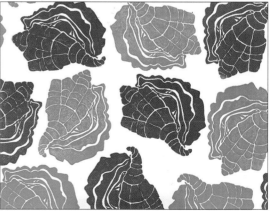

Two outline stamps prints. One consists of simple contours only (above) and the other includes detailed stippling (right).

A broad-surface stamp print.

Ready-Made Stamps

Commercially produced stamps are manufactured using a variety of materials. Most commonly, the *die,* which is the material into which the stamp image is etched, is made from a flexible substance such as rubber, plastic, or foam. Sometimes the die is affixed to a *mount,* or handle, which is usually made of wood, foam, or Plexiglas.

RUBBER STAMPS

From a material standpoint, rubber stamps are made in the greatest number of variations. The most widely available type of rubber stamp consists of a rubber die mounted on a thin foam cushion that is in turn attached to a wood handle. Rubber dies are also mounted on foam handles; this type is usually found in rubber stamp kits. A *roller stamp* is a rubber die mounted on a plastic roller, so that an uninterrupted pattern of images is printed as it is rolled over a surface. Rubber stamp images are made in a multitude of styles, to suit virtually every taste, interest, and project requirement.

DIE-CUT FOAM STAMPS

The dies of foam stamps are cut from a dense foam, then mounted on a foam or other type of handle. Because they are less expensive to produce, foam stamps can be made larger than most rubber stamps, and thus are appropriate for large-scale applications such as decorating walls and fabric stamping. Their softness and flexibility also make them easy to use on curved or rounded surfaces. In addition, many kits include assorted foam shapes and mounts that can be combined to create original stamp designs.

Rubber stamps come in an enormous variety of shapes, sizes, and image styles.

Because they are made larger than rubber stamps, foam stamps are suitable for use on walls as well as decorative and domestic fabrics.

Making Your Own Stamps

If you can't find a ready-made stamp image that suits your needs or personal taste, it's easy to create exactly what you want by carving your own. To get started, all you need is an image, which you can design yourself. If you're not entirely confident in your drawing or design abilities, you can copy or adapt an existing image from clip-art books, magazines, or other reference materials (such as a wallpaper or bedding pattern) to conform exactly to your project's specifications.

Many materials, including sponges, foam, potatoes and other produce, linoleum, printing blocks, and erasers, can be carved and combined or used alone to make artful stamp tools. Your image's degree of complexity will be the primary factor affecting your choice of stamp-carving surface. Generally speaking, sponge, foam, and potato stamps are best suited to simple, broad-surface images with minimal detail, while linoleum, printing blocks, and erasers can be carved more intricately to make detailed outline as well as broad-surface designs.

SPONGE AND FOAM STAMPS

When selecting a sponge for stamping, bear in mind that its density and surface texture will affect not only the kind of shape you can make, but the quality of the stamp print. For example, a dense synthetic foam sponge can be cut with a sharp knife to create simple geometric shapes, while a compressed sponge (a thin sponge that expands when moistened) can be easily cut with scissors into somewhat more elaborate shapes. In addition, the texture of a print made with an ordinary household sponge will look very different from one made with a lacy sea sponge. Simple precut foam sponge stamps can be found in art supply and craft stores.

Sponge and foam stamps can be used with virtually any type of ink or paint. Because these stamps are so absorbent, if you're working with a stamp pad you may need to load it with extra ink or paint.

Sponges can serve as stamps by cutting them into simple shapes.

POTATO STAMPS

By applying just a few simple carving techniques, a humble raw potato can become an outstanding stamping tool. Potato stamping, also known as potato printing, is one of the simplest forms of the craft, and has been used for centuries to create a range of decorative effects.

Begin by selecting potatoes that are large enough to accommodate your design. Depending on its size and complexity, an entire motif can be carved into a single potato half, or a single motif can be broken down into several elements, each of which is then carved into its own half. Create a paper pattern by tracing the motif on a piece of tracing paper and cutting it out with scissors. Cut the potato neatly in half and place the paper pattern on the cut potato surface. Use a craft or kitchen knife to cut as deeply as possible around the outline of the pattern. Working from the outer edge of the cut surface, carefully cut around the outline to remove the parts of the potato that you don't want to include in the print.

A metal cookie cutter provides a quick and easy alternative to tracing and carving. Simply press the cookie cutter deep into the cut surface, then use a sharp knife to cut around its outline and remove the excess. Simple details can be added with carving tools (see page 16 for a description of these).

Since a potato stamp begins to deteriorate when it is used repeatedly, resulting in a gradual decrease in print quality, it is recommended that potato stamping be restricted to small projects; for large projects, more than one potato should be carved with the same design.

Potato stamps work best with stamping and acrylic paints, mainly because they cover surfaces so consistently. When used with stamp inks, a potato stamp should be blotted thoroughly on a paper towel prior to inking.

Potato stamp essentials: Tracings and paper patterns of stamp motifs and a raw potato sliced in half to give it a flat carving surface.

Cut around the outline of the motif with a knife, then remove any excess by cutting in toward the shape. Use carving tools to add basic details, such as the veins in a leaf or the line that defines a flowerpot rim.

LINOLEUM, PRINTING BLOCK, AND ERASER STAMPS

Available at your local art supply store, linoleum, printing blocks, and erasers are the most widely used materials for carving complex stamp images, as they are relatively soft and easy to cut. Printing blocks, which are sold under the brand name of Speedball Speedy Cut, are similar in appearance to linoleum, but are softer and somewhat easier to carve. Although both rubber and plastic erasers can be carved into stamps, note that plastic erasers can be carved with more detail, hold shapes well, and are less prone to crumbling. The textures of all these materials can range from smooth to grainy; when selecting them, keep in mind how the texture will affect the character of your print. In addition, they are available in a range of sizes, though anything larger than an index card may need to be pressed with a paper or flower press, or weighted with something heavy like a stack of books, in order to achieve an even print.

Craft knives and carving gouges and tools (such as V-tools and U-tools, which are named for the shapes of the cuts they make) in a range of shapes and sizes can be used for cutting and sculpting. Narrow tools are used to incise outlines and details, while wider tools are used to carve away large areas.

You can draw your design directly on the surface, or you can trace a drawing on it using carbon or graphite paper. As with all stamps, printed images mirror, rather than duplicate, the stamp die, so remember to trace letters and numbers in reverse so that the prints will read correctly.

Linoleum, printing block, and eraser stamp essentials (clockwise from top left): a pencil with sheets of tracing paper and graphite paper (carbon paper can also be used), a printing block (mounted on wood), linoleum blocks, plastic erasers, and several cutting and carving tools.

Use a pencil to trace the outlines of the motifs on a sheet of tracing paper.

Transfer the motif from the tracing to the linoleum or eraser by sandwiching a sheet of carbon or graphite paper, treated side down, between the tracing and the carving surface, then retrace the lines.

Remove areas of the stamp surface that surround the traced areas with carving tools.

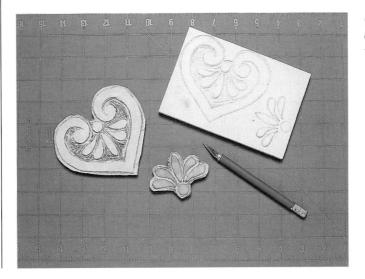

Cut out the completed stamp with a craft knife.

"FOUND" STAMPS

The art of stamping with objects that are not intended for printing has been around for centuries. Naturalists and herbalists once made prints of leaves and flowers to identify and classify plants. *Gyotaku,* a technique used by the Japanese in the early 19th century to document a catch by printing the likeness of a fish on paper, evolved into a fine art.

The possibilities are limitless. A wide range of "found" or "junk" objects can be used as stamps, particularly those with textured surfaces. Common household stamp finds include string, rice, or beans glued to a block of wood, wine bottle corks, corrugated cardboard, and sliced fruits and vegetables. An unusual product sold under the brand name of Penscore, which consists of sheets of specially treated foam, can be heated and impressed with a variety of objects, then used as a stamp.

Beautiful stamp prints can be made with ordinary objects.

Stamp Inks, Paints, and Pads

There are so many different kinds of stamping inks and paints on the market that it can be difficult to know which is best for a particular project. The factors to consider when choosing an ink or paint are the project surface, the stamping technique, the project's intended use, and whether it will need to be protected with a finish coat of varnish or polyurethane, as some inks or paints run or bleed when a finish is applied. Many manufacturers have developed stamp media that can be used on a variety of surfaces, so before you get started, read and follow label instructions carefully and test all of a project's elements on a scrap piece of the surface to ensure their compatibility. You might also experiment with traditional art and craft media such as water-based markers (see page 26), as well as nontraditional media such as bleach.

The fundamental physical difference between inks and paints is simply that inks have a more fluid consistency. Also, inks have a tendency to be absorbed by surfaces, whereas paints generally sit on top of them.

INKS

The five principal types of inks used for stamping are dye-based, pigment, embossing, fabric, and permanent. All of these are available as stamp pads in a variety of shapes, sizes, and colors (including combinations, such as rainbow assortments or seasonal themes); some are also sold in plastic bottles called *re-inkers,* which are used to either refresh dry ink pads or to ink uninked stamp pads (see "Making Your Own Stamp Pad," page 22). Most stamp pad surfaces are made of either felt or foam. Dye-based inks are most commonly paired with felt pads, while pigment, embossing, fabric, and crafting inks are usually manufactured with foam pads.

Generally sold in assortments of three or more colors, rainbow stamp pads come in a variety of color combinations.

Dye-based inks are usually manufactured with felt pads (right), while pigment, embossing, fabric, and crafting inks are commonly paired with foam pads (left).

Dye-Based Inks

Even if you're not an accomplished stamper, you've probably used a dye-based ink. These translucent, water-based inks are available on felt stamp pads in a range of sizes, from small 1-inch squares to large rectangles. Dye-based inks work on all types of paper, although their colors are most vibrant on white, glossy coated papers. Note that dye-based inks have a tendency to fade over time, particularly when exposed to light.

Pigment Inks

Thick, opaque, and slow-drying, pigment inks are found on foam stamp pads. These fade-resistant inks look rich and vibrant on wood, terracotta, and uncoated and colored papers. Because they are slow-drying, they can be used with embossing powders. In fact, pigment inks will not dry when used on coated papers unless they are embossed. You can also stamp fabrics with pigment inks and emboss them with clear embossing powder, although the surface of the print won't be raised and will feel slightly brittle.

Embossing Inks

Designed to dry slowly so that embossing powders will adhere to and fuse with a stamped image when heat is applied, embossing inks are available in clear and translucent formulations, and can be paired with either felt or foam pads. These glycerin-based inks can also be used as resists. For more information, see "Embossing," pages 39–40.

Permanent Inks

Permanent inks can be used on just about any stamping surface, and work especially well on paper, wood, and fabric. Their most noteworthy feature is that they won't run once they've dried, an important consideration when a protective finish must be applied to a stamped surface. Always check the manufacturer's instructions.

Fabric Inks

These inks are formulated specifically for use on fabrics, remaining soft and flexible after drying and ensuring washability. Note that some brands must be heat-set in order to be made permanent, so check the manufacturer's instructions before using. Depending on the type of fabric, a stamp print can be heat-set in a clothes dryer or by ironing the reverse side of the fabric. Fabric inks are also a great choice for wood and walls (two surfaces for which heat-setting is unnecessary), since they won't run or bleed when a protective finish is applied.

PAINTS

The two types of paint most commonly used for stamping are stamping paints and acrylic paints. Stamping paints are available in plastic bottles, while acrylics are sold in tubes, jars, and plastic containers.

Fabric inks can be used on hard surfaces such as wood and walls as well as on fabrics.

Stamping Paints

Stamping paints are the most recent addition to the stamper's creative arsenal. Developed to satisfy the needs of a broad variety of stampers, stamping paints can be used to stamp on fabric, wood, paper, and walls, and are available in numerous colors as well as metallics. These water-based paints have a longer "open" or drying time than acrylic paints (see below) and clean up effortlessly. Their extended drying time permits several colors to be applied to a stamp to create multicolor impressions, and the paints stay wet until the print is made. Stamp paint colors mix and blend easily, and can also be mixed with acrylics.

Acrylic Paints

Widely available in a rainbow of colors, acrylics are compatible with most stamping surfaces. These versatile water-based paints are most commonly used to basecoat wood projects, but can also serve as a stamping medium, though they must be handled quickly because they dry so quickly. Acrylics can be mixed or combined with an array of other media, including transparent glaze and crackling mediums, to create a variety of effects and surface textures. When mixed with *textile medium,* an additive that softens the dried paint film, acrylics can be used to produce washable stamp prints on fabric.

Note that latex paints, which are essentially the industrial equivalents of acrylic paints, can also be used for basecoating and stamping.

MAKING YOUR OWN STAMP PAD

If your preferred stamp medium is not available in a pad, or if you want to customize a multicolored pad for a particular project, you can quickly create a temporary ink pad by placing a layer of felt on a flat plastic tray or a piece of aluminum foil, then inking it with ink or paint.

Commercially manufactured uninked stamp pads, both foam and felt, are also available. Experimentation is suggested to ensure that a pad material is compatible with the ink or paint you've selected.

Acrylic paints can be used for basecoating as well as stamping on most stamping surfaces.

Customize a stamp pad by inking an uninked pad, or make one by layering a piece of felt over foil, then inking the felt.

Other Stamping Supplies

There are a number of tools and materials that stampers can use to enhance and embellish their art. Some are traditional crafting and sewing supplies, while others are on the cutting edge of art materials science, developed to satisfy the demands of enthusiastic stampers.

THE ESSENTIALS

Many of the items that make regular appearances on project materials lists are common household or office items that can be easily found in art supply, craft, stationery, and fabrics and notions stores.

Scissors and Craft Knife. You'll find these tools to be indispensable when cutting and shaping paper, fabric, and other materials. Small *scissors* are recommended for cutting paper, particularly when making the detailed cuts required for masks, paper patterns, and découpage. *Novelty-edge scissors,* including pinked, scalloped, and waved, can make whimsical edges on paper and fabrics. To avoid tearing papers when using a *craft knife,* make sure the blade is sharp.

Cutting Mat. A self-healing cutting mat protects your work surface when cutting with a craft knife. The mats that are ruled make measuring and alignment easy. A flat piece of cardboard similar to the type used as a backing for a tablet of paper is a good substitute.

Rulers. A *cork-backed metal ruler* is an essential accessory for cutting straight edges with a craft knife. In addition, a metal ruler's raised edge prevents ink from seeping under it when drawing straight lines with a marker. Sold in fabric and notions stores, a *clear plastic ruler* printed with grid lines is useful for marking measurements on both fabric and paper, and can also be used as an alignment tool for quick-cutting fabric with a rotary cutter.

Blank Newsprint. Sold in pads at most art supply and craft stores, sheets of blank newsprint are used to protect work surfaces and for stamping test prints. I usually work directly on the pad, then tear off the top sheet as it becomes soiled. When stamping garments and other fabric projects, insert a sheet or two of newsprint underneath or inside the item to prevent seepage.

Stamp Positioning Tool. This tool is designed as an aid for printing stamp images accurately, or for restamping incomplete or lightly stamped images. (See "Printing with a Stamp Positioning Tool," page 34.)

Tracing Paper. Tracing paper is used to transfer stamp designs from drawing paper to a stamping surface (sponges, potatoes, erasers, and linoleum) in preparation for carving, to create templates that for use with a stamp positioning tool (see above), and to protect paper surfaces during burnishing.

Post-it® Notes. Used primarily for creating masks (see "Masking," page 36), these sticky bits of paper come in various sizes. The recently introduced repositionable glues make it possible for you to create your own sticky notes from regular bond paper.

Embossing Heat Tool. Actually an adaptation of a paint-stripping tool, an embossing heat tool is designed to melt embossing powders by emitting very high heat with low air flow. It can also be used to weaken and soften glues. NOTE: This tool is not recommended for use by children under the age of 12 unless supervised by an adult. (See "Embossing," page 39.)

Glues and Adhesives. When choosing the "right" adhesive from the multitude of glues on the market, you'll need to consider your project's surface as well as its intended use. When necessary, the projects in this book specify the particular type required. Having some of the following glues on hand should satisfy the requirements of most stamping projects.

- *Tapes.* Several types of tape are used for stamping projects. Because its adhesive won't leave a residue, a *low-tack white artist's tape* is great for masking blocks or stripes on paper surfaces, and for positioning paper patterns and masks. *Double-stick tape* is good for layering papers when making stationery and greeting cards. *Blue painter's tape* is used to mask areas on wood furniture and walls, and as a guide for positioning paper patterns. (See "Masking," page 36.)
- *Glue pen and glue stick.* Stampers use *glue pens* to adhere papers, embossing powders, and glitters. The pen is usually fitted with a chisel tip that must be pushed down prior to use so that the glue will flow into it. The chisel tip is particularly suited to drawing borders, either freehand or with the guidance of a metal ruler. Use a *glue stick* (or double-stick tape) when gluing together heavy papers, such as for collaging and other layering techniques.
- *Glue guns.* A glue gun is used to adhere heavier papers and to attach small objects such as metal trinkets, buttons, raffia, and pieces of cardboard to various surfaces. Both glue guns and the long sticks of glue that are used to "load" them are available in several temperature grades, from low to high. Low-temperature glue guns and glues are appropriate for papers, while their high-temperature counterparts are suitable for wood and other sturdy materials. Check the manufacturer's instructions to determine which is right for your project.
- *Perfect Paper Adhesive™.* This product is an archival-grade acrylic glue used for projects in which the degeneration of materials should be avoided, such as photo albums, scrapbooks, and fine-art collages. It can also be brushed on certain papers prior to embossing, to protect papers and to prevent inks from being absorbed so that the height of an embossed print will be maximized. (See "Embossing," page 39.)

A selection of basic stamping tools: cutting mat, corked-back metal and gridded plastic rulers, standard and novelty scissors, Post-it Notes, craft knife, pencil, stylus, bone folder, craft and hole punches, stamp positioning tool, blue painter's tape, double-stick tape, low-tack white artist's tape, various glues, embossing heat tool, and glue gun.

Bone Folder. The point of a bone folder is used primarily for scoring and making sharp folds in paper, but can also be used to add texture to clay and soft metals or to turn the corner of a fabric project right side out. The flat end can be used as a burnisher, to strengthen the bond between glued papers. (Protect the paper's finish by covering it first with tracing paper.)

Stylus. This tool is useful for scoring paper, as well as for creating blind-embossed shapes when used with a brass or cardboard template and a light table. Like a bone folder, it can also be used as a texturizing tool on malleable surfaces.

Hole and Craft Punches. These versatile tools can be used to make simple stencils, stickers (simply punch some shapes out of sticker paper), and other interesting touches.

TOOLS FOR CREATING COLOR AND TEXTURE
Described on the following pages are some alternatives for adding color and texture to stamped images. Some, like watercolor, chalk, and pastels, are traditional fine-art media that have been used for hundreds of years; others, such as markers and embossing powders, were developed or introduced to the art and craft markets more recently.

Water-Based (Dye and Pigment Ink) Markers. These can be used to add color to a stamped print, as well as to ink a stamp by applying the color directly to the die. (See "Inking with Water-Based Markers," page 33.) Because their inks are water-soluble, they won't stain or otherwise damage a die. When working with other types of stamps, experiment to see how well the ink will transfer from the stamp to the project surface. These inks are best suited to stamping papers; as they are not lightfast, avoid exposing the stamped surface to light in order to keep the prints from fading. Water-based markers are available in several tip styles, including brush, fine, chiseled, and double-ended.

Permanent Ink Markers. This type of marker can be used to color in stamped prints but should *never* be used to ink a stamp die, as they stain permanently and will contaminate any colors used subsequently. In addition, they dry too quickly to be transferred from a die to the project surface.

Paint Markers. Paint markers are primarily used to accent stamped images by adding details or decorative hand-drawn flourishes. Because these paints are generally very dense and opaque, they tend to obscure detail when used to ink outline stamp dies directly or to color in highly detailed prints, and thus should be used primarily with simple broad-surface stamps. Paint markers are made in many colors and are offered in a variety of tip widths, such as chisel, bullet, and brush.

Textile Markers. These markers are used on fabric and wood to color and embellish stamped images. As with fabric paints, their colors do not run or bleed when a protective finish is applied over them. Like permanent ink markers, textile markers should not be used to ink stamp dies.

"Disappearing Ink" or Fade-Away Fabric Markers. This type of pen is used to mark sewing and stamping guidelines on fabrics. Depending on the fabric, the purple ink can remain visible up to several hours before it fades away. The ink can also be removed with a damp cloth or cotton swab.

Watercolors. Available in tubes, cakes, and pencils, watercolors can be used to add color to embossed prints or to prints stamped with permanent ink. In addition, a watercolor wash can be applied to a background prior to stamping. See page 55 for an example.

Acrylic Paints. Acrylics are used primarily in this book as basecoats for many wood projects, but can also be used for stamping (see page 22). They are available in a multitude of colors as well as metallics.

Stamping Paints. These opaque, water-based paints, which were developed specifically for stamping, feature a long drying time, which makes it easy to blend colors and to isolate specific areas of a stamp die. (See "Isolating Part of a Stamp Image," page 33.) In addition, they can serve as basecoat paints on a variety of surfaces.

Water-Based Glaze. A glaze is basically a transparent paint made up of only two of three essential paint ingredients; namely, binder and solvent. When the third ingredient, color, is added (in the form of paint or pigment), the glaze assumes that color while retaining its translucency. Glazes add color, texture, and depth to previously flat painted surfaces. Commercial water-based glazes, which can be purchased in paint stores, can be tinted with either acrylic or latex paints. Depending on the formulation, the surface finish can range from matte to high-gloss.

Antiquing Medium. This product, which is available in both water- and oil-based formulations, is used to impart an aged look to a range of surfaces, including paper and wood.

Colored Pencils, Chalks, and Pastels. If you like subtle, softly blended color, these "dry" media are good choices for coloring stamped prints. Much variation can be achieved by layering colors and combining them with other media such as markers. I like to use colored pencils over markers to create depth and shading.

Embossing Powders. Embossing powders are used in the printing industry to create *relief,* or raised, type and images with a glossy finish. To create a raised image with a stamp, you must use a slow-drying ink or paint (embossing and pigment inks and stamping paints are all appropriate) and a heat source (in the form of an embossing heat tool) so that the powder will bond with the ink and adhere to the project surface. Embossing powders are available in a range of granulations, from coarse to fine, and numerous colors and finishes, from glossy to textured. (See "Embossing," page 39.)

Embossing Pens. These slow-drying ink pens are used in conjunction with embossing powders. Available in several colors and in a variety of tip styles, they are used to create borders and add detailing to stamped images. If you want the ink color to remain visible, use clear embossing powder, as a colored embossing powder will obscure the color of the ink.

Glitters. Glitters can add luminescence to stamped images in an extensive range of colors, shapes, and textures. In contrast to embossing powders, glitters are adhered to surfaces with glue, so no heat is required.

Powdered Pigments. These materials can be used to create metallic, pearlized, and iridescent finishes on your stamped projects, either by brushing them on and sealing them with a varnish, or mixing them with inks, paints, or polymer clay. Make sure you take precautions when working with certain brands of powdered pigments. Note that Pearl Ex Powders by Jacquard, which consist of finely ground mica, are nontoxic and have no special handling requirements.

Gold and Metal Leaf. Gold and other metals, including copper, aluminum, and various alloys, have been used for centuries to ornament a range of surfaces. The basic procedure for gilding involves adhering extremely thin leaves of metal to a surface with a type of glue called *size*. Some types of metal leaf must be varnished to prevent tarnishing.

Puff Paint. Puff paints, which are sold under such brand names as Liquid Appliqué™, are used to add texture and dimension to stamp prints on paper and fabric. Available in an assortment of colors and usually equipped with a fine-tipped applicator, puff paint is applied to a print, allowed to dry, then treated with heat (either from an embossing heat tool or a hair dryer) so that the paint puffs up. If heated immediately, the paint will take on a rough "popcorn" finish; if allowed to dry overnight prior to heating, the finish will be smooth.

An assortment of tools and supplies for adding color and texture to surfaces and for applying and manipulating inks and paints.

TOOLS FOR APPLYING INKS AND PAINTS

The following is a list of tools for applying inks and paints, to ink stamp dies as well as to embellish and texturize project surfaces.

Paintbrush. Available in a wide array of sizes, shapes, and hair types, paintbrushes are used to coat surfaces with paint and varnish, to add decorative details to stamped prints, and to remove stray flecks of embossing powder before heat is applied.

Foam Brush or Sponge Roller. Comprised of a soft, absorbent sponge mounted on a stick or roller, a foam brush or sponge roller can be used to ink stamp dies and to apply inks and paints to project surfaces. The roller is also handy for making stripes on walls or furniture projects.

Wedge-Shaped Applicator Sponge. Included on the materials lists of most of the projects in this book, soft, high-density foam wedge sponges are used primarily to apply inks and paints directly to stamp dies (see page 32), but can also be used to sponge on or texturize a wet basecoat prior to stamping.

Stencil Brush. This short, round, stiff-bristled brush is designed specifically for stenciling, to distribute paint evenly and to help prevent it from oozing under a stencil.

Stippling Brush. A stippled surface exhibits a soft, subtle texture, which is produced by manipulating a wet coat of paint or glaze with this type of dense, compact brush.

Sea Sponge. Yet another texturizing tool, a sea sponge can add interest to surfaces when used to apply color.

Combing Tool. Use this decorative painting tool to create a combed, striped, or striéd design on a freshly painted surface.

Brayer. A brayer is a rubber roller mounted on a handle. Available in several roller widths and in varying degrees of elasticity, brayers are most commonly used to ink stamps (they are particularly well suited to linoleum blocks) but are also used to create colorful patterned backgrounds, most typically on glossy coated papers.

Lay the brayer down on the flat side of its handle so that the roller will still turn. Select an assortment of water-based markers (do *not* use permanent ink markers), then spin the roller with one hand as you hold the tip of each marker against it to draw lines, varying their width and the spaces between them as desired. Breathe on the roller to moisten any inks that may have dried, then roll it on the surface. The brayer can also be inked by simply rolling it on a rainbow ink pad. Experiment with other patterns and ink combinations.

Making a Print

A stamp print's appearance depends on three variables: how and with which medium its stamp is inked; whether the print is colored, and, if it is, which medium and colors are used; and the texture of the stamp surface. In this section, the steps involved in making a clean, clear stamp print are summarized, from inking a stamp with various tools to printing with a stamp positioning tool. This overview is provided to help you determine which techniques will work for a particular project with a minimum of trial and error.

If you're working with a rubber stamp, note that it's sometimes necessary to trim away excess rubber with a craft knife in order to remove areas that you want to avoid inking. This step is particularly important for large rubber stamps, which require a bit more pressure during printing. Another way to avoid inking areas of a rubber stamp that you don't want visible in a print is to carefully ink the die with a small raised stamp pad.

If you're using a purchased foam stamp, you may want to trim away some of the backing so that it's easier to position the stamp accurately on the project surface.

INKING WITH A STAMP PAD

A stamp pad can be used to ink a stamp in one of two ways: By pressing the stamp die on the pad, or by tapping the pad on the die. In general, felt pads, which are relatively hard, require a bit more pressure, while the softer foam pads are less likely to overink a die when just lightly tapped on its surface.

The stamp pad's raised surface makes inking any stamp die, large or small, a nearly effortless undertaking. An economical way to collect a wide variety of colors, small pads are extremely versatile, as they can be used to ink areas or elements of a die with specific colors, to isolate part of a stamp design (see page 68 for an example of the isolating technique), and to blend colors directly on the die (see page 33).

Small ink pads can be used to ink an entire die (near right) or to color specific elements (far right).

INKING WITH A BRAYER

If you're inking a stamp with a single color of stamp paint, acrylics, or bottled ink, inking with a brayer is probably the best way to go. Pour a little bit of paint or ink on a small piece of glass (use the glass from an old picture frame), then roll the brayer across its surface until both the brayer and the glass are covered evenly. Ink the stamp by rolling the brayer across the die, or you can use the glass as a stamp pad of sorts. This method of inking can be used with any type of stamp.

To ink a stamp with a brayer, coat the roller evenly with ink or paint, then roll it across the surface of the stamp.

INKING WITH A BRUSH OR SPONGE

Like brayers, paint or foam brushes and various sponges can be used to ink stamps with fluid inks and paints. Either a piece of glass or a paper, plastic, or Styrofoam plate can serve as your "palette"; just pour a little of each color on its surface so that you can load your tool easily.

Traditional paintbrushes are particularly useful for inking stamps—even fairly detailed ones—when making a multicolor print. Load the brush with color, then apply it to the die by brushing a particular area or element of the motif. In contrast, foam brushes are better suited to inking large broad-surface stamps.

Although many different kinds of sponges can be used to ink stamps, dense sponges are the most likely to yield even coverage of the die. A highly textured sponge would give you an irregular-looking print, but this may be the look you're after. The flat side of a wedge-shaped applicator sponge is used to ink the stamps of many of the projects in this book. These sponges are easy to use, readily available, and can be used for multicolor as well as one-color stamping. Load a sponge by tapping its flat side in ink or paint, then blotting off the excess on another area of the palette. Ink the stamp by patting the sponge on the die.

Use a foam brush to ink large broad-surface stamps when working with fluid inks and paints.

Wedge-shaped applicator foam sponges can provide even coverage on more detailed stamps.

INKING WITH WATER-BASED MARKERS

Inking a stamp with water-based markers allows you to apply a different color to each area of a die, creating a multicolor image with just one impression. This technique is particularly effective for color blending. (See "Blended Effects," below.) Water-based markers can be used to ink any type of stamp. Use only water-based markers to ink the rubber dies of your stamps, as permanent marker inks are absorbed by stamp surfaces and will contaminate any colors you use afterward.

After coloring a die with water-based markers, reactivate any inks that may have begun to dry by breathing warm, moist air on the die before stamping.

Many broad-surface stamps are specifically designed to be inked with water-based markers.

BLENDED EFFECTS

There are many projects in this book in which blended color is an integral part of the design. When inking a die directly with two colors, apply the lighter of the two first, then add accents in the darker color. To achieve a gradual blend, gently apply the lighter color at the point where the two meet. The blended color of the pear prints on page 11 (center) was created by scumbling yellow and orange stamping paints directly on the die.

ISOLATING PART OF A STAMP IMAGE

As it applies to stamping, the word "isolate" means to ink and print only a specific part of a stamp die. This technique maximizes the versatility of your stamps, as several distinct images can be printed with one stamp. For instance, if the foliage on a fruit stamp is just right for one of your projects but you hadn't planned on featuring fruit, there's no need to purchase or carve a separate leaf stamp. Simply ink the portion of the die that you want to print.

PRINTING WITH A STAMP POSITIONING TOOL

Using a stamp positioning tool makes it possible to print a stamp image precisely where you want it. Typically made of clear plastic, stamp positioning tools come in several varieties, but most look like either a T-square or an L-square. Note that this method of printing only works with stamps that are mounted on rectangular blocks, so if you plan to use a stamp positioning tool with an unmounted stamp, you'll need to mount it on a block before you begin.

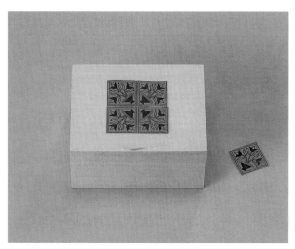

Make paper patterns of the stamp image, then arrange them on your surface.

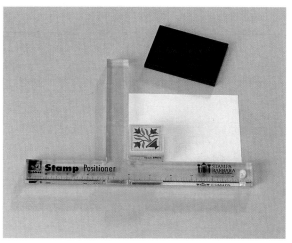

Make a template of the image by aligning the corner of a piece of tracing paper with a right-angle corner of the stamp positioning tool, then inking and stamping the image. Make sure that the sides of the block are also aligned with the right angle of the tool.

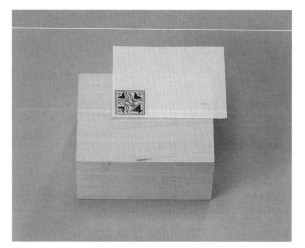

Place the tracing-paper template over the paper pattern so that it aligns exactly, or put it wherever you want to print the stamp image.

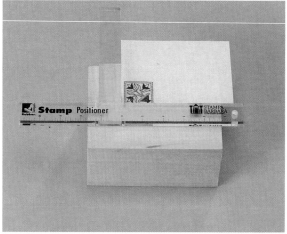

Align the right angle of the stamp positioning tool with the edges of the tracing-paper template. Make sure you use the same right-angle corner that was used to stamp the template.

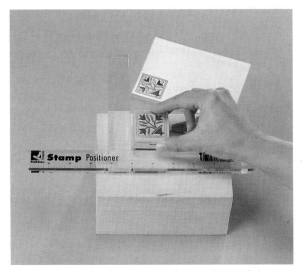

Keeping the tool in place, remove the template and the pattern, ink the stamp, then stamp the image directly on your project by aligning the block in the corner of the tool. The orientation of the template and the inked stamp should be the same.

The completed stamp print. To correct a weak print, place the template over it, then align the right-angle corner of the stamp positioning tool with the corner of the template. Remove the template, ink the stamp evenly, and reprint the image by aligning the sides of the block with the right angle of the tool.

The finished project.

Masking

Masking is a technique in which a stamp print, or part of a print, is *masked,* or covered with a paper cutout of itself, to protect it from subsequent stampings. It is used to create the illusion of depth by making one print appear "behind" another; to create a border, panel, or background; to isolate part of a stamp image; or to stamp one print inside another (called *reverse* or *mortise masking).*

To make a mask, stamp a print on a Post-it note so that the sticky backing at the top of the note is at least partially on the back of the image. The backing keeps the mask firmly in place until you remove it. (You can make your own "sticky notes" by printing the stamp on a piece of lightweight paper and applying a repositionable adhesive to the back.) Carefully cut around the print just within its outline to keep from leaving a blank area around the edges of the masked print when overstamping.

Available at art supply stores, masking fluid or frisket is a form of liquid latex that can also be used for masking on most surfaces (check the label instructions before using). Brush it on a print or over a specific area; once dry, it forms a rubberlike barrier that protects the surface beneath it. After stamping is complete, simply peel away the mask.

CREATING DEPTH

Stamp and color a print as desired, let it dry, then cover it with its mask. This protects the masked print so that other images can be stamped around and over it. After the mask is removed, the first print will appear to be in the foreground of the stamped surface, while any others will appear to be behind it.

(Top left) Stamp the print on the project surface, then prepare its mask. (Top right) Cover the print with the mask. (Bottom left) Stamp another print over the masked one. (Bottom right) Remove the mask. The first print appears to be in front of the second.

MASKING BORDERS AND PANELS

Both tape and scrap paper cutouts can be used to mask areas on a stamping surface to create panels, borders, and decorative edges. In the example below, left, two separate applications of blue painter's tape were used to create a central panel of red daisies and a surrounding border of yellow daisies on a pillow cover. In the frame shown below, right, two paper cutouts—one for the yellow panel around the picture area, and one for the green border—were used to stamp and paint a wood frame.

Lengths of blue tape were used at full width to define a central panel for the red daisies.

After the red daisy prints dried, the tape was removed. Two sets of tape, both cut to half-width, were used to protect the edges of the central panel to define the outer edges of the border for the yellow daisy prints.

As a finishing touch, thin squiggles of green paint were used to define each stamping area after the tape was removed.

The mask for the inner panel was cut from the center of a sheet of paper with a craft knife. The resulting border mask was placed on the frame and the panel was painted and stamped. The border mask was removed and the panel mask was put in place so that the border could be painted and decorated.

MORTISE MASKING

A *mortise* is a hole or slot into which part of something else fits. Mortise masking is used to stamp one print inside another, or within a particular shape. Preparing a mask for this technique is similar to creating a stencil. Stamp a piece of paper or a Post-it note, then carefully cut out all or part of the print with a craft knife to remove it from the paper. Place the mask over its stamped version; when a second print is stamped over it, it will "fit" inside the first.

The design of this papier-mâché box (top) is deceiving in its complexity. Each side was basecoated with a different color and its lid was painted red. A broad-surface heart stamp was printed on each side of the box in a contrasting color, then stamped in several colors on the lid so that the tip of each heart points to the center. Stencil-style masks of the heart stamp were prepared, placed over each of the prints, and a checkerboard stamp was printed over them in a contrasting color (bottom). When the masks were removed, the checkerboard prints appeared within the contours of each of the hearts.

Embossing

Thermal embossing produces a lustrous, raised image by stamping a print with a slow-drying ink (either embossing ink or pigment ink), sprinkling it with embossing powder, tapping off the excess, then heating it with an embossing heat tool. The embossed print can be left as is or further embellished with markers or paints. Embossing is typically done on paper and wood, but can also be done on fabrics, which must be stamped with pigment inks and embossed with clear embossing powder. Note that the surface of an embossed fabric print will be flat rather than raised and will have a slightly brittle texture.

Inks and embossing powders can be combined in several ways. Embossing inks, which are either transparent (clear) or translucent (lightly tinted), are made to be used with colored powders. Pigment inks, whose colors are opaque, should be used with transparent or translucent powders so that the ink color remains visible. When a colored powder is applied over a colored ink, the final image takes on the color of the powder.

Some interesting textural effects can be achieved through experimentation. For example, a transparent embossing ink used with a transparent or translucent embossing powder will produce a beautiful, glasslike print. Try matching the colors of the ink and powder to that of the stamped surface; for instance, white ink and powder on a white surface, or black ink and powder on a black one.

Embossing powders can also be blended. Ink and stamp the image, then sprinkle powder on specific areas of the print. Tap off the excess. Sprinkle another color over the remaining areas of the print, then tap off the excess and melt the powders with an embossing heat tool.

(Top left) Stamp the print with embossing or pigment ink. (Top right) Sprinkle the print with embossing powder. (Bottom left) Tap excess powder off the print onto a sheet of paper. Shape the paper into a funnel to return the excess powder to its container. If necessary, use a small clean paintbrush to remove any stray flecks of powder before heating. (Bottom right) Apply heat with an embossing heat tool until the powder melts.

EMBOSSED RESISTS

Embossed prints can also be used as resists on white glossy coated papers. Emboss a print with embossing ink and transparent embossing powder. Use a stamp pad or marker to ink the flat side of a wedge sponge with dark ink, then brush or pat the color over the embossed print. Blot the image with a clean dry paper towel to pick up excess ink. The contrast of the white of the transparent embossed print against the colored background creates a radiant glow.

PREPARING SURFACES FOR EMBOSSING

Though most papers can be embossed without having to prepare them in any special way, tests should be conducted on fragile papers, which may be affected by the high temperature of the embossing heat tool, as well as on handmade papers, whose porousness may reduce the height of an embossed print because they absorb most of the embossing ink. One way to avoid such pitfalls is to coat these papers with a transparent glue such as Perfect Paper Adhesive (see page 24). Simply brush a thin layer of glue on the paper and let dry. This step seals the paper, preventing inks from being absorbed.

Wood, both finished and unfinished, can also be embossed, though the powder takes longer to melt than it does on paper. When applying heat to finished wood, move the embossing heat tool over prints continuously to keep from damaging the surface, and avoid applying heat to areas where the powder has already melted.

You can also try embossing sheets of heat-resistant transparent acetate (the type used for overhead projectors), then use them to make cards and shadow boxes.

As the dark ink is sponged over it, the white of the transparent embossed print will become visible.

Before embossing fragile or absorbent papers, seal them with a thin layer of glue.

Creating Depth and Dimension

There are several stamping techniques that rely on the interplay between light and shadow, or light and dark values, to create an illusion of dimension and depth.

OVERPRINTING

In its simplest form, *overprinting* prints one image directly over another; however, with this technique, no masks are used. Depending on the desired effect, the two prints can be in similar or contrasting colors, and either precisely aligned or slightly out of register. An example of the latter can be seen below, as well as in the Overprinted Floral Placemat project on page 104, in which potato prints are overprinted with linoleum prints slightly off-center.

To make the wrapping paper shown here, the image was printed in a light color. The stamp was cleaned while the first prints dried, then the second set of prints were overprinted slightly out of register in a darker color. For an interesting effect, stamp the first image in a darker color, then overprint it in a lighter one.

DOUBLE-INKING

Another multiple-stamp technique, *double-inking* entails inking a medium-sized to large broad-surface stamp twice. Begin by inking the die of the large stamp with color, either solid or blended. Use contrasting colors to ink a second stamp—one that's smaller and more detailed than the first—then print it directly on the die of the first. The result is a highly complex and elaborately colored dimensional print.

These beautiful ornamental flower pots were created using the double-inking technique.

SHADOWS

When a print seems somewhat flat and uninspiring, it may benefit from the addition of a shadow. The following are some simple techniques for adding depth to a stamped image.

Outlining. To make a simple shadow, use a marker or a paintbrush to outline one side of a print in a medium gray. When outlining several prints, be consistent about the positions and widths of the shadows, in order to represent only one implied light source. Inconsistently placed shadows will create visual confusion.

Masking and Overprinting Slightly Out of Register. This technique, in which a print stamped in a light to medium color (the foreground image) is masked and overprinted with a dark one (the shadow), is best suited to broad-surface stamps.

Outlining. Although these three strawberry prints are oriented differently, the positions and widths of their shadows are consistent, indicating that the light source is above and to the right in all three instances.

Masking and Overprinting. Ink and stamp the print with a light to medium color, then make a mask (see page 36) and clean the stamp.

Cover the first print with the mask. Ink the stamp with a dark color, then print it slightly out of register, either to the left or right and/or higher or lower than the first, depending on the position of the implied light source. You can "eyeball" the position of the second print, or use a stamp positioning tool to place it precisely (see page 34).

COLOR AND DESIGN

Once you're familiar with the material choices available to you and have a grasp on how to employ them, it's time to explore another set of options—those of color and design. Sometimes such decisions are made before a project is even begun, because one or more of its particulars—for example, the color or shape of the surface, or the intended location or recipient—suggest, and in some cases even prescribe, color scheme and layout.

But when the circumstances of a project don't suggest a definitive approach, what should be a process of pleasurable experimentation becomes an agonizing chore. This section is calculated to minimize the distress of indecision and feelings of confusion by equipping readers with the vocabulary and skills they need to acknowledge, then to successfully express, their ideas.

Making Sense of Color

Most people respond to color on an emotional level, gravitating toward their favorites and avoiding or even dismissing others. This strategy can make it easy to put together a particular room or project, but using the same colors over and over again can make for a monotonous decor. Also, there are times when it seems impossible to make a decision, either because too many colors appeal to you, or because you just don't seem to like one more than any others.

When you get "stuck," you can sort things out by referring to a *color wheel,* and by having a basic understanding of the color terminology reviewed below. Using these tools doesn't mean that you have to make every color decision on an intellectual basis; on the contrary, having an understanding of color theory can only make you feel more comfortable about using your intuitive color sense.

The color wheel illustrates the relationships among the three *primary colors*—yellow, red, and blue—whose position within the color wheel creates an equilateral triangle. All other colors can be made by mixing the primaries. Each of the three *secondary colors* is a mixture of two primaries: yellow + red = orange; red + blue = violet; and blue + yellow = green. The six *tertiary colors* are made by mixing a primary color with an adjacent secondary; for example, red + orange = red-orange; yellow + green = yellow-green. Excluded from the color wheel are black, white, and the range of grays in between. These are referred to as *achromatic colors,* which simply means that they contain no color at all.

Every color can be described in terms of four properties: hue, value, intensity, and temperature. All color is perceived within the context of contrast of any or all of these characteristics; these contrasts can be manipulated to create visual emphasis. A variety of other factors also affect color perception, such as the quality of the light by which a color is viewed, the extent of the area to which a color is applied, and the color and texture of the background or surface on which a color appears.

- *Hue* is the characteristic of a color that designates it as red, yellow, blue, and so on. For example, the hue of ochre is yellow-orange; the hue of turquoise is blue-green. The most vivid contrast of hue occurs between two *complementary colors,* which lie directly opposite one another on the color wheel. When complementary colors are placed side by side, each intensifies the other.
- *Value* refers to the relative lightness or darkness of a color, as it relates to white, black, or the range of grays in between. A color is described as light, medium, or dark in value. A color's value can be changed by mixing it with white, black, or gray, or by adding a lighter or darker color to it. A *tint* is made by mixing a color with white; a *tone* is made by mixing a color with gray; and a *shade* is made by mixing a color with black. Dark or low-value

colors are perceived to be heavier in weight than light or high-value colors. High-value colors appear to expand space, while low-value colors appear to compress it. A color outlined with black or a low-value color looks more saturated than when it is outlined in white or a color of lighter value.

- *Intensity* refers to the relative brightness or dullness of a color. Pure colors are the highest in intensity. The primary colors are the purest on the color wheel; the secondaries are less intense because they are mixtures. A color of medium intensity appears dull when compared to a pure hue, but will appear brighter when compared to a low-intensity color.
- *Temperature* is a somewhat subjective appraisal of color. Reds, oranges, and yellows are associated with warmth, while blues, greens, and purples are considered cool. Warm colors tend to advance or move toward the viewer within a composition, while cool colors tend to recede. Cool colors expand space, while warm colors tend to compress it.

A standard color wheel is divided into twelve hues: three primaries, three secondaries, and six tertiaries.

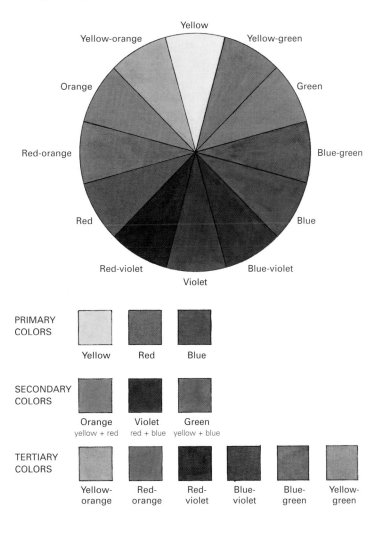

PRIMARY COLORS

Yellow   Red   Blue

SECONDARY COLORS

Orange   Violet   Green
yellow + red   red + blue   yellow + blue

TERTIARY COLORS

Yellow-orange   Red-orange   Red-violet   Blue-violet   Blue-green   Yellow-green

Informed Color Choices

The perspective from which you approach your color "problem" depends not only on the stamping project itself, but whether the room in which you are planning to locate your project has a discernible *color scheme*. A color scheme is a group of colors used in any creative undertaking, from decorating a room, to planting a flower garden, to putting together an outfit.

The best way to start is with some examples. There are many standard palettes based on the color wheel; a few of these are shown below and opposite. Rather than following each color scheme to the letter, use them as general guides to choosing colors.

Analogous color schemes include two to five adjacent colors on the color wheel. These make the most harmonious palettes because they all share a common color. This decorative box and matching candlesticks, painted in metallic acrylic paints in blue-green, blue, and blue-violet, illustrate an analogous color scheme. Touches of embossed gold and rhinestones heighten their sparkle.

Monochromatic color schemes use just one hue in a range of tints, shades, and tones. In this example, yellow (the curtains) and ochre (the glazed wall) comprise the monochromatic palette for a stamped project. The design of the pillow, which is painted and stamped in an unusual drybrush style, features four squares of color. One of the squares echoes the color scheme of the room, while the remaining squares provide maximum contrast in color and temperature by including its complement (blue) as well as another set of complements (red and green).

Complementary color schemes consist of two colors that lie directly opposite one another on the color wheel. In this example, an antiqued wooden frame provides the background for the contrast between the warm pink of the hibiscus and the cool green of its leaves.

Split-complementary color schemes *include a color from one side of the color wheel and two colors on either side of its complement. These gold-embossed boxes, which were covered in pastel mulberry papers, combine the palest red and violet flowers with yellow-green leaves.*

Triadic color schemes *use three colors that are equidistant from one another on the color wheel. One example of a triadic palette would be red, yellow, and blue, as shown on this stamped quilt.*

Tetradic color schemes *include four colors, which are always two sets of complements. These combinations are created by placing a square or rectangle over the color wheel and rotating it to yield different groups of colors. This grouping of pillows and boxes features a muted tetradic palette of yellow-orange, green, red, and blue-violet.*

Designing a Surface

There are several ways to approach the design of a project's surface, which involves how stamp prints are arranged or organized. The main factors are the dimensions and shape of the surface, which influence the number and size of the images you've chosen as well as the spacing between them. Each surface gives you a different set of options. For instance, a decorative box can feature one large or several small widely spaced prints; a pillowcase can be embellished with a border of small images, a central design, or an all-over pattern; a room can be stamped randomly or at a regular interval, or just a corner can be brightened with a sprinkling of images.

PATTERNS AND REPEATS

Basically, a pattern is the arrangement of images on a surface, either one element repeated several times or several different elements. A pattern can be a simple vertical or horizontal line of a single element, or a complex grouping of disparate elements.

A *repeat* is a pattern whose elements occur in a continuous flow, at regular intervals and without interruption. A repeat pattern can consist of a single design element or a combination of several different ones, and can be any shape or size, as long as the structure of the pattern is constant.

There are two basic types of repeat: square and half-drop. A *square repeat* is laid out so that each unit of the design matches up with the side of the next one, to create a continuous pattern both vertically and horizontally. A *half-drop repeat* follows the same principle as a square repeat, except that the adjacent design units are dropped halfway down the length of the overall pattern.

The spacing and orientation of elements can dramatically affect pattern formation. Spacing is often dictated by the parameters of a project's surface (see page 54), while orientation is generally limited only by the image itself. Within either type of repeat pattern, images or elements can be spaced and oriented in a few different ways. The distribution of images within a pattern is referred to as either *packed* (with very little space in between) or *spaced* (in which so much space is left between images that the color and texture of the project's surface become principal elements of the design).

In addition, images can either be *tossed* (oriented in different directions) or *set* (all oriented in the same direction).

Two patterns whose elements are widely spaced and oriented in a set layout, one in a square repeat (top) and the other in a half-drop repeat (bottom).

STRATEGIES FOR PATTERN DESIGN

There are two easy methods for designing patterns. Both provide a means for experimentation, so that the final result is attractive, balanced, and enhances the surface.

Grids. A particularly helpful device for constructing accurate repeat patterns, a grid provides a framework for organizing images at fixed intervals. Some simple grid formations are shown below. Each can be adapted in scale and/or proportion to conform to specific projects.

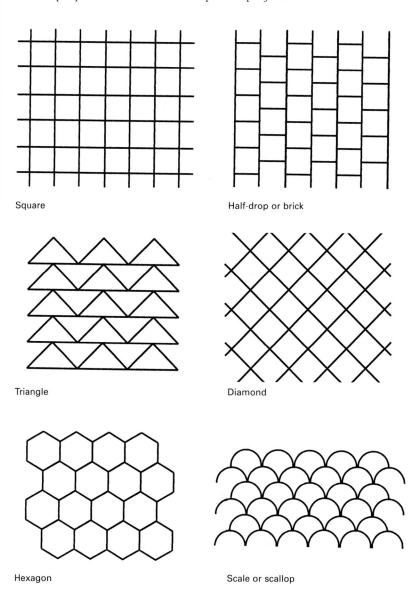

Square

Half-drop or brick

Triangle

Diamond

Hexagon

Scale or scallop

Scrap Paper Patterns. Scrap paper patterns can be used to design layouts for both random and repeat patterns as well as other types of compositions. To prepare scrap paper patterns, stamp the image or images several times on scrap paper and cut the prints out. (If you have access to a photocopy machine, you can make duplicate patterns by making several copies of one print.) Position the patterns on the surface of your project and use them as guides to determine placement, spacing, and orientation. Consider whether masking would be appropriate by overlapping patterns. Experiment with creating large, complex motifs by combining several small images. Lengths of low-tack masking tape fashioned in loops keep patterns in place and can be repositioned without damaging most surfaces.

Before stamping this bird of paradise fabric print (left), paper patterns of the flowers and foliage were arranged on the muslin ground to determine a pleasing layout (above).

WORKING WITHIN SPECIFIC PARAMETERS

There are times when a project's physical constraints can simplify decisions about where stamp images should be placed.

Borders. Depending on the project and the look you're after, a border requires a little planning. Of course, a border on a square or rectangular surface would be approached and carried out differently from a wall border, which follows a room's perimeter at a particular height (see page 79). A balanced border on a square or rectangle can be designed by following a fairly standard set of guidelines. Begin by placing images at the corners, then center images between them. Place other images between these, again so they are evenly spaced. If there seems to be too much space among the various images, it may be necessary to add smaller ones that coordinate with the first set, or perhaps you can mask the images to achieve a continuous, balanced border.

Circles. Round objects such as plates and clocks can sometimes offer virtually foolproof layout solutions. Centering a large motif is just one strategy. If the surface has a defined rim or edge, you may want to begin by placing the principal images there, at noon, three, six, and nine o'clock, then evenly spacing smaller, secondary images between them.

The layout of this circular plate was begun by stamping a checkerboard print on the slightly raised rim. A rabbit was stamped in the center, then flowers were positioned above and below it and on either side following a clockwise orientation. The word "bunny" was handwritten between the flowers, the letters curving to echo the shape of the surface.

Stamping and Other Crafts

Stamps are versatile creative tools, and can be combined with a wide range of other crafting techniques.

Paper Crafts. Collage (see page 130) and papier-mâché (page 134) are excellent ways to display stamp images. In an unusual twist, the furniture collage project on page 92 stamps thin slivers of mica instead of paper.

Stenciling. Like stamping, stenciling can be used on a variety of surfaces. Creating a stencil is similar to preparing a mortise mask (see page 38).

Decorative Painting. This adaptable craft is used on a variety of surfaces throughout this book. *Sponging*—either by applying paint with a sponge, or by using a sponge to texturize a wet basecoat—is a great way to add interest to a surface before enhancing it further with stamp prints. *Color blocking* masks off bold shapes with stencils or masking tape to create striking blocks of color. An example of color blocking appears on page 22.

Watercolor. Watercolors and stamps can be combined in a number of ways. Embellish a watercolor composition with stamp prints. If you're planning to enhance stamp prints with watercolor, use permanent or waterproof stamp inks so they won't run. Color selected areas of a print with watercolor pencils or water-based markers, then use a moistened paintbrush to draw the color throughout the image. If you don't have any watercolors on hand, load a moistened paintbrush by stroking it on a dye-based inkpad.

After each pink and blue bunny was stenciled on white sheeting, the stencil was left in place so that the prints could be stamped with flowers.

To make this découpage screen, several images were stamped on watercolor paper with permanent ink and allowed to dry, then painted with watercolors.

STAMPING SURFACES

Before starting a project, it's important to have at least a general idea as to how the intended surface you've chosen will interact with its other elements. You could approach each surface on a trial-and-error basis, but that could easily end up being wasteful, time-consuming, and, above all, frustrating.

This section provides some fundamental guidelines for working with a wide range of surfaces: paper, the original stamping surface; wood, both finished and unfinished; timeless fabrics such as cotton and muslin, as well as new possibilities like velvet; unfired and prefired clay surfaces, including ceramicware, terracotta, and glass; the popular craft medium of polymer clay; and even such unlikely options as metal, leather, and suede, which in fact are well-established stamping surfaces.

Paper

Paper is the first surface that most people think of for stamping. In addition to the traditional selection of machine-made products, including coated, uncoated, textured, tissue, lace, origami, vellum, and cardboard, the surge in popularity of handmade papers, some of which include plant and cloth fibers or recycled materials, has yielded an astounding assortment of papers for stampers. Papers can be found at a range of suppliers, from stationery, office supply, art supply, and craft stores, to specialty outlets such as rubber stamp retailers and paper and party supply stores.

Your choice of paper will depend on the project. Before making a decision, you must consider whether a paper's physical characteristics—size, weight, color, and surface texture—will suit the ways it will be used in a project; for instance, whether it will be cut, torn, folded, or otherwise manipulated; how it will affect the appearance of a particular ink or paint; and how it will respond to the adhesive you plan to use. Also, before making a major investment, it's advisable to buy a small quantity of any paper you're considering to make sure it's compatible with all of the materials and techniques involved in a particular project.

Keep in mind that papers can be used for more than just stationery and gift wrap. Explore the creative potential of beautiful paper crafts, such as collage and papier-mâché (see pages 130 and 134 for examples).

A stunning selection of papers that can be used in stamping projects.

This unusual, easy-to-assemble kid's chair is made of sturdy corrugated cardboard. Here, acrylic paints were used for both basecoating and stamping.

Wood

Wood items, from furniture to smaller pieces such as frames, boxes, and shelves, both finished and unfinished, can be decorated with stamps. The effect you're aiming to achieve will have a bearing on the ink or paint you use and its method of application. Pigment, fabric, and permanent inks as well as stamping paints and acrylics are all compatible with wood, but you should check the manufacturer's instructions before applying any medium to a project. (Dye-based inks and water-based markers are not recommended for use on wood, as they may transfer to hands when the object is handled, or run when a final varnish is applied.) For coloring stamp prints on wood, use textile markers or colored pencils (*not* watercolor pencils), neither of which will smear once they're applied. Unless a glossy finish is desired or you expect that the finished project will be handled frequently, it isn't necessary to protect the prints with a glaze or sealer. For information on embossing on wood, see "Preparing Surfaces for Embossing," page 40.

PREPARING UNFINISHED WOOD FOR STAMPING

If the surface of your wood item is rough, sand it until smooth, then wipe it thoroughly with a tack cloth to remove any sanding dust. To prevent ink from bleeding into the unfinished wood, you must seal it before stamping. (Unfinished wood can be embossed without prior sealing.) If the wood grain of your piece won't compete visually with the stamps you're planning to use, you can either spray it very lightly with a matte-finish acrylic spray sealer and stamp on it as is, or brush on a coat or two of water-based stain before sealing to modify the color of the wood without obscuring its grain.

You can find a wide range of unfinished wood items at many art supply, crafts, hardware stores, and lumber yards, as well as at garage and tag sales.

Note that a heavy coat of sealer may prevent stamping ink from adhering to the surface and make it impossible to color in the image. If you prefer to stamp on a solid color, simply paint your sanded piece with a light coat of stamping, acrylic, or latex paint, all of which also act as sealants.

STAMPING ALREADY FINISHED WOOD

While it's generally unnecessary to alter a wood finish in preparation for ink or embossing powder, the slick surfaces of glossy wood finishes are the most difficult to work with, as stamps are inclined to slip. When working on a glossy finish, you should "kiss" the wood with the die, using a very light touch to apply it to the surface.

There are many different kinds of finished wood objects that can be used as stamping projects, including picture frames, mirrors, storage boxes, shelves, and serving trays.

Fabric

Creating original designs on fabric is a wonderfully satisfying way to use stamps. An increasing number of fabric inks and paints, some of which were developed specifically for stamping, has made it easier to find just the right colors. Along with the classic stamping surfaces of cotton, cotton blends, and muslin, just about any fabric can be stamped and stitched, including linen, silk, and velvet (see "Decorative Stamping Projects," pages 100–122, for some examples).

Generally speaking, smooth-weave, minimally textured fabrics in light colors yield the clearest prints, but interesting effects can be attained by stamping on highly textured and/or dark fabrics. Avoid highly detailed images when stamping on textured fabrics, as at least some of the detail is likely to be lost. If you plan to use a dark fabric, test the ink or paint on a scrap first, since the color of the fabric will affect the appearance of the color of the ink or paint. Even commercially printed fabrics can be stamped. For example, you can stamp a stripe or plaid by arranging the stamp prints between or within stripes, or decorate a fabric that features large blocks of colors with an intricate stamp design. Regardless of its color or design, it's a good idea to experiment on scrap pieces of a fabric before starting any project, so that you can determine whether its various elements—stamp image, ink or paint, fabric, and colors—will actually give you the look you're hoping to achieve.

For those projects that will inevitably require laundering, such as wearables, pillows, table linens, and curtains, fabrics must be machine- or hand-washed prior to stamping in order to remove sizing, dried according to label instructions, then pressed well to straighten the grain and eliminate wrinkles. If you don't plan to wash a project after you've stamped it, then you don't need to wash it beforehand.

If you're not an accomplished stitcher, you can find forms and blanks for items such as floorcloths (shown here), pillows, and placemats at fabric and notions stores and other retail outlets.

This plain white cotton pillow cover was embellished with stamped crazy-quilt patches of several understated tone-on-tone miniprints.

61

DIRECT STAMPING

The term "direct stamping" simply means to ink and stamp an image right on the fabric surface. (For a description of an "indirect" stamping technique, see "Working with Heat Transfers," below.) Always work on a flat, stable surface, which you should protect with a few sheets of blank newsprint to absorb any ink or paint that may bleed through the fabric. Depending on the inks or paints you use, you may need to lift the stamped fabric periodically to make sure that the newsprint isn't sticking to the reverse side. If you're working on a two-sided project such as a T-shirt or purchased pillow form, insert a flat piece of cardboard between the front and back to prevent bleed-through. Check the manufacturer's instructions to see whether (and by what means) the ink or paint should be heat-set once the prints have dried.

WORKING WITH HEAT TRANSFERS

Heat transfers generally appeal to people who feel a little intimidated about the prospect of direct stamping. Once a project has been stamped with ink or paint, it's difficult (if not impossible) to remove a mistake unless it's covered with a scrap of fabric. Using heat transfers reduces the potential for error somewhat, because you can place images precisely where you want them, and prints are always complete. In addition, heat transfers make it possible to enlarge and reduce motifs.

Many photocopy retailers carry the special paper required for this technique, and have machines that make color as well as black-and-white copies. Stamp your prints on white bond or cardstock, then have them copied onto the shiny side of the transfer paper, either at same size (100 percent) or enlarged or reduced to your specifications. Don't limit yourself to stamping a single print on one sheet of paper. You can make several prints (of one or many stamps) on the same sheet, or make prints, play with sizes on a copier, then cut them out and position them all on a single sheet of white bond before copying them onto transfer paper. To transfer prints to the fabric, cut them out, place them printed side down, then iron the back of the paper.

Because the heat transfer process creates a mirror image of a stamp print, if your stamp includes numbers or letters you can print it on clear acetate instead of white paper, then photocopy the back of the acetate print so that it can be copied onto the transfer paper correctly. If you want the final fabric prints to show two distinct orientations, copy some of the stamp prints on a copier with a mirror-image feature. An example of this can be seen in the finished fabric shower curtain (shown opposite, bottom), whose fish are swimming in two directions.

Ink the stamp and print it on white paper. (Clean stamps thoroughly when changing ink or paint colors.)

If desired, enlarge and/or reduce the prints to make a variety of sizes, or change their orientation with the mirror-image feature. Cut out all of the prints and group them on a single sheet of standard-size (8½- × 11-inch) white paper, then copy them onto the shiny side of a sheet of transfer paper.

Carefully cut out the transfer prints, leaving about an ⅛-inch margin around each.

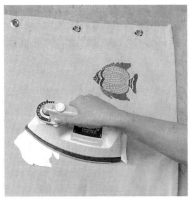

Place a transfer print face down on the fabric. Set your iron on "cotton blend." (Do not use steam.) While exerting pressure, iron the print for about 15 to 20 seconds. Peel the print off the fabric surface, working from bottom to top. If the transfer doesn't peel away easily, iron it for about 10 seconds more. Repeat with the remaining prints.

The completed fabric shower curtain. Note that a separate plastic liner is required for this type of curtain.

"EMBOSSING" VELVET

Velvet embossing, which is also referred to as heat stamping, uses a rubber stamp to impress a print into the velvet's nap, but without ink, paint, or embossing powder. The back of the fabric is misted with water, the damp area is placed nap side down on the die, then pressed with a dry iron. Foam, sponge, and potato stamps are not appropriate for this technique because they can't withstand the heat of the iron. Use a broad-surface stamp, as details can be obscured in the velvet's pile. Rayon velvet, which is relatively inexpensive, is best suited to this technique; cotton velvet (also inexpensive) and silk velvet (generally the most expensive) are also good choices. Start by making a test print on a scrap of velvet. If the area of the die surrounding the image interferes with the print, it may be necessary to cut it away with a craft knife before you begin.

Velvet embossing basics: A broad-surface rubber stamp, a fine-mist spray bottle filled with water, an iron, and a length of velvet.

Place the rubber stamp die side up on a hard, flat surface. Lay the velvet nap side down over the die, then lightly mist the area over the die with water.

Apply an iron set on "permanent press" to the area and hold for approximately 20 seconds. Keep the steam vents from pressing into the rubber by placing a sheet of bond-weight paper between that part of the iron's surface and the fabric.

The completed print. The print's metallic sheen is not the result of ink or embossing powder, but is caused by the light that reflects off the surface of the velvet's nap.

Terracotta, Pottery, and Glass

Recent developments in art materials technology have produced several new media for surfaces such as terracotta tiles, glass, and unfired ceramic blanks. Several different kinds of paints and glazes are now available, each of which has its own set of application and finishing techniques. When choosing a medium, you must consider whether the project you're stamping will be purely decorative or used and handled extensively.

When stamping slick or very smooth surfaces, the amount of pressure applied to the stamp should be minimized to keep the die from sliding. When a stamp does slip, simply wipe away the misprint with a damp paper towel.

KILN-FIRED GLAZES

Sold in art supply stores and ceramics studios, bisqueware glazes are designed to be used on all manner of materials that require firing in a kiln, including unfired earthenware, porcelain, and other ceramicware. When the glazes are fired they become fused with the project's surface, which then becomes safe for use with food and is able to withstand exposure to water, abrasive cleaning, and repeated handling. These attributes make the glazes appropriate for dishes, vases, and tiles that will be affixed to walls in high-traffic areas. Since their colors change considerably during the firing process, many ceramics studios display charts that indicate what the glazes will look like after they're fired to assist you in making your selection.

Ceramics studios carry an overwhelming assortment of unfired bisqueware blanks, from entire place settings to vases and tiles. Shown at left is a lidded heart-shaped box that was sponged with a light pink glaze prior to stamping. Foam stamps are particularly well suited to stamping curved surfaces, as they are pliable enough to be shaped to their contours.

PAINTS AND INKS FOR TERRACOTTA, GLASS, AND OTHER PREFIRED SURFACES

Designed for use on terracotta, glass, and previously fired ceramics and porcelain, there are several brands of paint that don't require kiln-firing. Instructions for application and finishing vary widely, so label directions should always be carefully observed. Some require that three different materials be applied—an undercoat to prime the slick surface, the paint itself, and a protective sealant—while others must be heat-set at relatively low temperatures in a home oven. Glass and prefired ceramics can also be stamped with acrylic and stamping paints, which must be sealed with a water-based varnish. Because these media are intended exclusively for use on purely decorative projects, they won't survive heavy traffic or rigorous cleaning, and should *never* be applied to the interiors of plates and containers used for food.

Terracotta can be stamped with ink as well as paint, but because it is very porous, in most cases it must be sealed with a light coat of acrylic spray sealer or paint to keep the ink from bleeding into it. The only exception to this is fabric inks, which will not bleed or run. Pigment inks can be used successfully on terracotta, and are permanent once dry. Dye-based inks should be avoided completely, as they will bleed into the surface of clay even after it's been sealed. If a glossy relief image is desired, use pigment inks with translucent embossing powders or embossing inks with opaque powders. While none of these materials requires sealing unless a glossy finish is desired, be aware that stamped and embossed terracotta items are purely decorative. For example, decorated terracotta tiles shouldn't be installed on floors or on surfaces that require more than an occasional cleaning with a damp sponge, and plastic liners should be used in stamped or embossed terracotta pots.

An unfired item can be stamped with bisqueware glazes and then fired, which permanently fuses the glaze to the surface (the vase, candy dish, and grape plate are examples), or fired and then stamped with ceramic, acrylic, or stamping paints, none of which require firing (the artichoke tile was decorated in this way). Glass, which should not be fired (either before or after stamping), is also stamped with the latter.

Polymer Clay

Polymer clay is a plastic-based material composed of particles of polyvinyl chloride (PVC) suspended in a plasticizer. The clay is soft and moldable at room temperature; when heated, the PVC particles fuse into a hard, durable plastic. Polymer clay has become very popular because it's baked (properly referred to as *cured*) in a home oven instead of fired in a kiln. Sold under various brand names, such as Sculpey, Fimo, and Cernit, this extremely versatile material can be embellished with stamps before curing, either with or without ink. Polymer clay comes in an array of beautiful colors and in special finishes such as metallics and granite, all of which can be mixed easily. You can use white or a neutral color if you prefer to finish your project with paint after it is baked, which is useful if you're trying to match colors precisely.

Before you can begin, the clay must be *conditioned,* or kneaded until it is pliable. Then use a rolling pin, brayer, the sides of a cylinder-shaped container, or your hands to roll the clay into a sheet approximately $1/8$ to $1/4$ inch thick, depending on the project. If desired, the sheet can be cut into shapes with a craft knife or cookie cutters, but this step can also be done after the clay has been stamped. Note that any tools used with polymer clay should *never* be used to prepare food.

If you're planning to stamp the clay without ink, choose a stamp with deeply etched images or one that's made from a material firm enough to make a clear impression. Keep in mind that this technique produces an *intaglio,* or incised impression, which simply means the raised areas of the die that are normally used to make a print on a flat surface are pressed into the soft clay surface, and the surrounding areas are slightly raised.

To make this polymer clay frame, white and gold clays were each rolled into sheets, then the gold was cut into squares and the white was cut into rectangles before being imprinted with stars and swirls. The shapes were cured, allowed to cool, and the white pieces were painted with red acrylic. All the shapes were then lightly coated with red pigment powder, then varnished front and back before being glued to a cardboard frame.

Experimentation will guide you in selecting the best stamps for stamping clay, and a little practice will help you determine how hard to press a stamp into the clay to obtain a clear impression. If excess surface area on the stamp interferes with the image, trim it away with a craft knife.

Stamps can also be inked and used to make prints on uncured clay. Pigment and permanent inks as well as acrylic paints are recommended for this purpose. Other inks are not compatible—specifically, there are problems with bleeding and running—and their colors are not as vivid on this particular surface.

Depending on how the clay will be used in a project, you might trim away excess following the contours of the print, or cut it to create a border around the print in a defined shape. You can heighten visual interest by using tools such as a stylus to texturize the clay that surrounds the prints. Follow the manufacturer's instructions for curing, which can be adjusted to allow for the thickness of your project. (Do not try to reduce curing time by increasing oven temperature above recommended levels, as burned polymer clay emits poisonous fumes.) After the clay has been cured and allowed to cool, it can be painted with acrylics or stamping paints.

Cured clay can also be embossed, but it's important to roll the clay out evenly before baking so that its surface will be as level as possible.

The cured and embellished shapes can be assembled to create a wide range of decorative items for the home as well as personal accessories such as jewelry and buttons. In addition to the picture frame shown on page 67, polymer clay is used in this book to make the "hardware" for a chest of drawers (see page 88) and to create decorative ornaments for terracotta flower pots (page 142).

The polymer clay leaves used to decorate the terracotta flower pots project (see page 142) were stamped without ink as well as with green pigment ink.

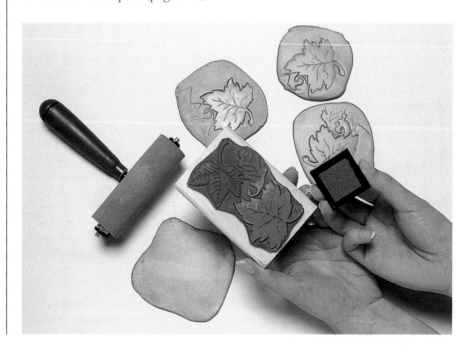

Metal

Sold at many hardware, art supply, craft, modelmaking, and rubber stamp retailers, thin sheets of copper, brass, and tin can be stamped to create ornamental embellishments and unusual projects.

PRINTING

Ink a stamp with permanent ink, print it on a metal sheet, then let dry. (Acrylics and stamping paints can also be used, but they must be finished with a protective varnish so they won't flake or chip when handled.) Because the surface of the metal is slick, exert a minimum of pressure on the stamp when making a print. Taking care to avoid touching sharp edges, carefully cut the print out with an old pair of scissors (the metal will quickly dull the blades on a new pair), then smooth its edges with a small metal file. The completed ornaments can then be used to embellish decorative items, or fastened to metal findings to make jewelry.

EMBOSSING

Metal can be embossed with embossing or pigment ink and colored embossing powders. When melting the embossing powder with the embossing heat tool, you can guard against burning your fingers on the hot metal by wearing gloves or holding the sheet with a pair of tongs, then letting it cool before handling it again. For an example of embossed metal, see the metal-trimmed mirror project on page 146.

Metal can be embossed as well as printed. Because metal conducts heat, you may find it necessary to wear gloves or hold the sheet with a pair of tongs.

HAMMERING AND PUNCHING

Begin by stamping a print on the back of a metal sheet with permanent ink, or by stamping the print on a sheet of sticker paper, cutting it out (leaving about an 1/8-inch border), then adhering it to the back of the metal. Pad your work surface with a thin piece of foam or a computer mousepad, then lay the metal right side down on the pad. Use a ball stylus, a large needle, an empty ballpoint pen, or the sharp point of a bone folder to trace the outline of the print. Accent the print's details and/or background by pouncing or piercing the metal with a stylus or needle (to simulate hammered or punched metal) or by "drawing" freehand designs. Cut around the completed piece with an old pair of standard or novelty-edge scissors. The right side of the metal can then be colored with a variety of media. Examples of this technique are shown below.

The traditional metalworking techniques of hammering and punching metal can be combined with stamping to impart dimension to a metal surface. These images were colored with metallic and permanent markers and rub-on metallic paste.

Leather and Suede

Leather and suede are available to stampers in a variety of forms. At art supply and craft stores, these materials are typically packaged in kits for making small items such as frames, keychains, and wallets, their surfaces ready for embellishment. For larger projects, such as the suede lamp shown below and the leather portfolio project on page 150, they can be purchased by the yard at leather supply stores and from mail-order sources. These suppliers also carry specialized tools and products, including sewing equipment, decorative punches, and glues.

Although these treated animal skins differ only in surface texture, that difference raises some important stamping considerations. For instance, while leather can benefit from a light moistening with water prior to stamping in order to make it a little more pliable and receptive to ink or paint, suede discolors or stains when it comes in contact with water. Also, smooth leather can be embossed but suede cannot, as the embossing powder will adhere not only to the embossing or pigment ink but will cling to the napped surface. Stamp prints can be made with success on both leather and suede using fabric or crafter's inks and acrylic and stamping paints.

Stamp prints should be protected with a waterproof finishing spray specially formulated for either leather or suede, or both. In addition to being sold in shoe stores, these products are also available at art supply and craft stores under a variety of brand names, including Leather Sheen.

The striking suede lampshade on this accent lamp features dimensional leaves stamped using one of the shadow techniques. (See "Masking and Overprinting Slightly Out of Register," page 43.)

71

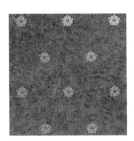

STAMPED INTERIORS

Even if you're not at all intimidated by stamping a small surface, it's likely that the prospect of stamping an entire room—not only its scale, but the expectation of its permanence—will at least give you pause.

In this section, the entire procedure of stamping a room is described, which includes systematically analyzing its layout, architectural elements, and contents in order to make an enlightened decision about color and stamp motif; making a detailed sample of the proposed design; then executing the design, whether it's an all-over repeat pattern, an engineered design, a continuous or freeform border, or a wreath. By employing essentially the same techniques that are used for walls, floors can also be embellished with stamps.

Assessing a Room

You've decided that you want to decorate a room with stamps, but where do you begin? The first step in the process is to objectively assess the room's elements, in order to determine its focal point(s) and how the style and arrangement of its furnishings will affect your decisions about color and motif. Since a room's architectural features are usually its most compelling, you can start by taking an inventory:

- *What is the general layout? Is it large, small, long, or wide? What are its dimensions? What is the ceiling height?* Depending on their color and spacing, large motifs may overwhelm a small room, or one with a low-pitched ceiling; small motifs may "get lost" or appear annoyingly "busy" in a large, airy one.

- *How many windows and entrances are there, and how do they organize the space?* The way in which windows and entrances "break up" walls will dictate whether it makes sense to stamp an all-over pattern, horizontal or vertical borders (or both), or an "engineered" design (see below).

- *Are there any moldings—a baseboard, chair rail, picture molding, or crown molding?* These elements, which lead the eye around a room's perimeter, are excellent guides for aligning horizontal borders. (See "Borders," page 79.)

- *Is there a fireplace or other dominant element, such as a major window grouping, a bay or bow window, or an arched entrance?* Such a feature can serve to support an *engineered design,* which is a grouping of one or more motifs, either freeform or patterned, that provides emphasis and interest. An engineered design can furnish charming detail in an otherwise empty or nondescript area; a sprinkling of motifs in a corner—stars, clouds, or even a freeflowing vine—is just one example. Such a design can also help integrate an element that somehow seems out of place, or that would require an enormous effort to change or remove it, such as the cement planter featured in the project on page 123.

If a room has virtually no outstanding features, you can use the dominant wall in the room, which is opposite the primary entrance, as the starting point for stamping. A horizontal border or an all-over pattern would be worked from the center of that wall out toward both corners.

In general, the contents of the room—furniture, accessories, and so on—will provide a secondary source of guidance. If, however, the room's architectural accents are sparse, you will need to rely more heavily on this aspect, perhaps making the dominant piece or arrangement of furniture the focal point of a room. Most importantly, the furnishings will suggest possible color schemes as well as the theme and scale of the motifs.

Although choices of color and motif are largely a matter of personal taste, it is possible to approach the task somewhat methodically. Evaluate whether the current decor has a distinct style, such as country, traditional, or modern, or reflects a particular historical period. Since people often acquire furnishings and objects over time and from a variety of sources, a mix of styles and/or periods, or an *eclectic* look, is not uncommon. In that case, look carefully at the colors, patterns, and scale of the motifs in the fabrics of the furniture and curtains. It isn't necessary to match all of their characteristics exactly; however, it's important to at least complement what's in the room to avoid visual chaos. It's usually best to start "safe," experimenting with comparatively small motifs rather than large ones.

MAKING SAMPLES

Once you've made preliminary decisions about color, motif, and layout, it's time to make a few samples. A sample can be extraordinarily helpful, particularly if you'll be painting a room prior to stamping your design or executing a faux finish that you have little or no experience with, and can give you an opportunity to ensure that all of your paints and inks are compatible. Last but not least, a sample can save you from the discouraging and time-consuming chore of painting over what was supposed to have been a "completed" finish.

If you'll be painting or executing a faux finish prior to stamping, make your sample on a large (at least a 20- × 30-inch) surface. You can purchase foamcore board, illustration board, and other supports appropriate for making samples at an art supply store.

In this tiny dining room, a small fleur-de-lis was stamped in gold to accent a collection of framed prints and mirrors. A larger motif would have overwhelmed the scale of the room. (See the project on page 126 for specific instructions.)

It's essential that the surface of the sample be prepared so that it mimics that of the intended wall, because the character of the wall surface will significantly affect the type of stamp image you choose. Outline or detailed broad-surface stamps are best suited to smooth surfaces but are a poor choice for textured surfaces such as stucco, on which fine lines will print unevenly and details will almost certainly be lost. Use simple broad-surface images on textured walls.

When painting the sample's basecoat, use the paint you're planning to use for the wall; that way, color and sheen will be accurate. Most walls can be painted with latex paint, which is quick-drying and available in a range of sheens, most commonly matte or flat, eggshell or satin, pearl, semigloss, and gloss. Semigloss and gloss sheens require a bit more care when stamping, as the dies may slide on the slick surface, especially if too much pressure is applied. Sometimes letting the ink or paint set for a few seconds on the die before stamping can alleviate this problem.

WORKING WITH PAPER PATTERNS

Once you've painted a sample you're satisfied with, or if you're planning to stamp the walls without painting them first, make scrap paper patterns of the stamp motifs you've selected. (See page 53 for instructions on how to prepare scrap paper patterns.) Since you'll be evaluating color as well as placement, it's best to stamp each one individually, or to make color photocopies, than to make black-and-white copies from an original print.

Affix a loop of low-tack masking tape to the back of each pattern, then begin positioning them on your sample or wall. By experimenting with placement and spacing, you'll be able to concentrate on developing certain layouts while ruling others out. During this step, which is especially important when working with more than one motif (or when one is large and the others small), you may also decide to eliminate or add a motif. When using just a single motif, you'll find that large ones typically need more generous spacing, while smaller ones can be spaced more closely. If you're trying to establish a repeat pattern, begin by following your visual instincts—do what feels right or looks good first—then adjust the spacing and placement of motifs to devise a consistent repeat. Because the sample is limited in size, the paper patterns must be transferred to the wall prior to stamping, so that the layout can be adjusted to fit the actual surface.

It's a good idea to live with your samples and/or paper pattern layouts for at least a few days before making your final decision. You may decide that your design requires additional work, either by amplifying or toning down what's there, replacing motifs, or starting over from scratch. If after a week you're still pleased, proceed to the next step. If you're stamping an all-over repeat pattern, you'll need to mark a grid (see opposite); if you're stamping a border, you'll be establishing guidelines with low-tack masking tape (see page 79).

Marking a Grid for a Repeat Pattern

Before you begin marking your stamping grid, you should be completely happy with the way your paper pattern layout looks on your wall. Then make sure that the spacing between motifs within a repeat is consistent.

Regardless of the design, your first guideline will be a vertical. The simplest way to mark an accurately straight vertical line on a wall is to attach a plumb line at the ceiling. (Ask someone to help you do this.) The plumb line is aligned over a vertical arrangement of motifs within the repeat, which should be positioned at or near the center of the dominant wall. Begin removing the paper patterns one by one, very lightly marking the center point of each one directly on the wall in pencil or chalk. (If you feel that the plumb line is in the way, you can indicate its guideline with low-tack masking tape, then remove it.) Use a ruler to measure the distance from one of the marks along the guideline to the center points of adjacent motifs, from side to side and top to bottom. Use these measurements to cut a cardboard rectangle.

- *To mark a square repeat,* align one side of the cardboard with the vertical guideline and one of its corners with the center point of a motif.
- *To mark a half-drop repeat,* place the cardboard on the diagonal so that the vertical guideline intersects the top and bottom points, which should each be touching the center point of a motif.

Very lightly mark the four corners of the rectangle in pencil or chalk. Repeat, repositioning the cardboard along the entire length of the guideline first, then at the pencil or chalk marks, until the entire wall is marked. These marks will serve as the guides for stamping your prints. Remember to gently erase each pencil mark or dust off the chalk mark right before stamping a print.

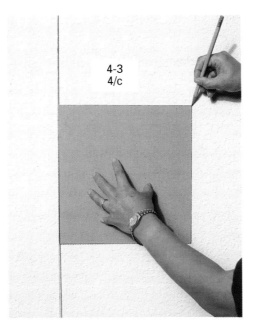

4-3
4/c

Use your premeasured cardboard rectangle to mark your repeat. For a square repeat, which is shown here, align one side of the rectangle with the plumb line and one of its corners with the center point of a motif. For a half-drop repeat, align the rectangle on the diagonal so that the plumb line intersects two of its corners, which should each be touching the center point of a motif. (See page 126 for a wall project featuring a half-drop repeat.)

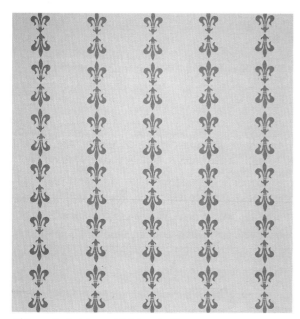

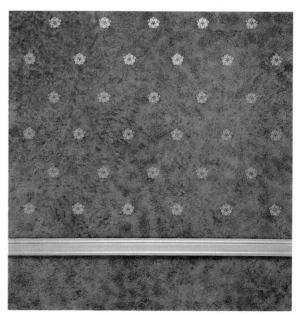

This vertical stripe, which is actually a square repeat, features fleurs-de-lis in a two-way layout.

A half-drop repeat stamped in gold metallic acrylic paint over a background sponged in dark green.

This half-drop repeat is based on a painted diamond grid. The wall was basecoated in a light taupe and allowed to dry. Painter's tape was applied in diagonals to mask off alternate diamonds before sponging on a darker taupe. After the paint dried and the tape was removed, the stars were stamped in copper acrylic paint at the diamonds' intersecting points.

Borders

There are two types of borders. The most popular is the *continuous border*, in which a consistent repeat runs the perimeter of a room at a specific height.

Use a tape measure to calculate how high from the floor you want the border to be. Mark this point with a pencil. Do this at several intervals along the width of the wall. To make a guideline for stamping your prints, affix low-tack masking tape to the wall along the pencil marks. Use the carpenter's level to make sure the tape is straight, adjusting its position as needed. (This is important, as floors and walls are not always perfectly plumb.) If you need a guideline against which to align the tops of your prints, add a second line of masking tape at the required point above the first, again using the carpenter's level to ensure that it's straight.

Freeform borders, which are intentionally less precise, use one or more individual motifs to create a design. The motifs are stamped more or less randomly, their positions varied to satisfy the stamper's personal taste. When stamping a freeform border, which should never appear rigid or static, it's recommended that you avoid using paper patterns or a masking tape guideline. If you use paper patterns to develop the design, use them only for general reference rather than as an inflexible template. If you feel uneasy stamping without a guideline, very lightly mark the wall with pencil or chalk. Allow your composition to develop slowly, working on it for a day or two, then letting it sit for a few days before resuming work. Let your creativity flow freely.

Once you've set up guidelines for your continuous border with low-tack masking tape, you can mark them in pencil to indicate spacing and position of motifs. The repeat pattern shown here was first worked out on a sample using paper patterns, which made it possible to ascertain exactly how the tape should be marked for the entire wall. The large scroll was stamped in alternating directions first (top), then a pair of leaves was added to fill the space between the scrolls (bottom).

Shown here are two examples of freeform borders. (Top) The dimensional effect in the border was achieved by stamping both grapes and foliage with a fadeout technique, in which a stamp is used to make several prints without re-inking, resulting in a variation in value that suggests depth. The vine was added last, using a brown paint pen. (Bottom) Use alphabet stamps to personalize a wall and make a statement. Here, an enigmatic observation by author Gertrude Stein is complemented with stamped roses.

Wreaths

A stamped wreath makes a beautiful accent over a mantelpiece, headboard, sideboard, or other relatively low-lying room element or piece of furniture over which a picture or mirror might normally be hung. Like borders, wreaths can be either precisely planned or freeform, depending on your taste and existing decor. The example shown in the step-by-step photographs below has characteristics of both.

There are a couple of ways to make a reasonably accurate circle as a stamping guide.

- If you have a bowl whose diameter is the same as the proposed wreath, place it bowl side down on the wall, then lightly trace its circumference with chalk.
- To make a cardboard template, tie a string that is equal in length to the wreath's radius to a piece of chalk. Fasten the other end of the string to the cardboard, then draw the circle by keeping the string extended to its full length. Cut around the circumference of the template, then affix it to the wall with double loops of low-tack masking tape. Lightly trace the template with chalk.

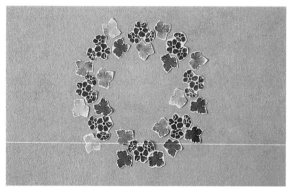

After chalking a circle on the wall, use paper patterns to determine the arrangement of the flowers and foliage.

Leave the patterns in place until just before making a print. Stamp all of one image's prints before stamping others.

If desired, add freehand details with a marker or brush.

The completed wreath.

Floors

Many of the decorative stamping guidelines for the vertical surfaces in a room can also be applied to floors. Designs can feature geometric shapes or repeats that frame or accentuate a specific area (as shown below), as well as random groupings, such as a scattering of leaves. A stamped floor can also help solve decorating problems by camouflaging ugly or rough spots or by breaking up a solid floor.

When properly prepared, both wood and concrete make excellent stamping surfaces. In any case, make sure the surface is scrupulously clean by eliminating all dust, wax, and soap residue prior to stamping. Because floors are subject to constant abuse, it's recommended that housepaints formulated for outdoor use or for specific surfaces (such as concrete) be used for basecoating.

Protect your stamp prints by applying two to three coats of water-based polyurethane, which is available in a range of sheens, or acrylic floor polish, which protects painted surfaces while allowing air to penetrate. Apply the finish over the stamp prints only, or to the entire floor.

When stamping a geometric design, mask off shapes with low-tack masking tape.

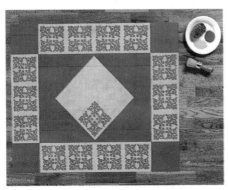

Once the basecoat is dry, stamp the prints section by section, working one color at a time.

The completed floor.

DECORATIVE STAMPING PROJECTS

This section features stamp projects for every home decorating need, demonstrating just some of the potential applications of image, color, design, and technique. Although complete materials lists and step-by-step instructions are provided so that each project can be duplicated exactly as it is shown, readers are encouraged to use the projects as inspiration for designing and crafting their own accessories, linens, bedding, furniture, and stamped environments, either to satisfy the requirements of an established decor, or to help define a style for a space in need of a distinctive look.

Checks-and-Cherries Garden Set

MATERIALS AND SUPPLIES

Projects

Unfinished wood end table with apron (tabletop dimensions: 18 × 23 inches)

Unfinished wood birdhouse (Walnut Hollow #11118)

Foam Stamps

Checkerboard (61010)

Cherries (61044)

Stamping Paints

(For basecoating and stamping)

Ivory

Bright red

Black

Hunter green

Seminole green

Miscellaneous

Fine sandpaper

Tack cloth

1/2-inch and 1-inch paintbrushes

Wedge-shaped applicator sponges

Scrap paper

Scissors

Ruler

Pencil

Rubber eraser *(to erase pencil lines)*

Plastic eraser *(for the square stamp)*

Synthetic-bristle varnishing brush

Water-based polyurethane, semigloss finish

*T*he classic checkerboard pattern, consisting of alternating squares in two contrasting colors or values, coordinates with practically any motif. In the two feature projects, black-and-white checks are paired with sprigs of bright red cherries to transform an unfinished pine table and birdhouse into cheerful decorative touches for the garden or sunroom.

By adjusting the color scheme and combining checks with several floral motifs, you can dress up a small-scale table-and-chairs set with a few coats of paint to make a special child a unique place to sit and play.

TABLE

1. If necessary, sand the table in the direction of the wood grain until smooth, then wipe it lightly with a tack cloth to remove all sanding dust.
2. Basecoat the tabletop and apron with ivory paint. Apply red paint to the legs. Let dry.
3. To create a paper pattern, ink the checkerboard stamp with black paint, stamp it on scrap paper, and cut out the print. Repeat to create about a dozen patterns. Position the patterns in the center of the tabletop to make a border.
4. Use a ruler and a pencil to lightly mark the outer parameters of the scrap paper border. Remove the patterns. Ink the checkerboard stamp with black stamping paint, then stamp the border by aligning the side of the stamp with the pencil marks. Let dry, then gently erase the pencil marks.

Position the patterns to make a border.

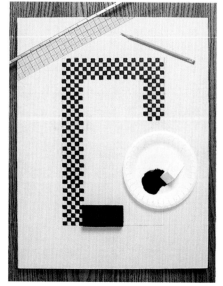

Outline the border with a pencil, remove the patterns, then stamp the prints.

5. Ink the cherries portion of the cherries stamp with red, then blend the two greens on the foliage. Stamp cherries prints around the checkerboard border and three cherries in its center, alternating their orientation as you go. Let dry.

6. Stamp the checkerboard in black on all four sections of the table apron. Dip the tip of the paintbrush handle into the paint to add ivory polka dots to the legs. Reload the handle for each dot. Let dry.

7. Finish with two coats of polyurethane. Let the first coat dry before adding the second.

BIRDHOUSE

1. If necessary, sand the birdhouse until smooth, then wipe it lightly with a tack cloth.

2. Basecoat the base and roof of the birdhouse with red paint. Paint the body of the house with ivory paint. Let dry.

3. Ink the cherries stamp as noted above in step 5, then print the cherries randomly over the body. Let dry.

4. Stamp the roof with the checkerboard in black. Let dry.

5. Cut a square from a plastic eraser the same size as one of the squares in the checkerboard stamp. Ink it with black paint and stamp it around the front of the birdhouse.

6. Use the handle end of the paintbrush as described above in step 6 to add ivory polka dots to the front of the roof and base. Let dry.

7. Finish with two coats of polyurethane. Let the first coat dry before adding the second.

Stamp the perimeter of the front of the birdhouse with a square cut from a plastic eraser.

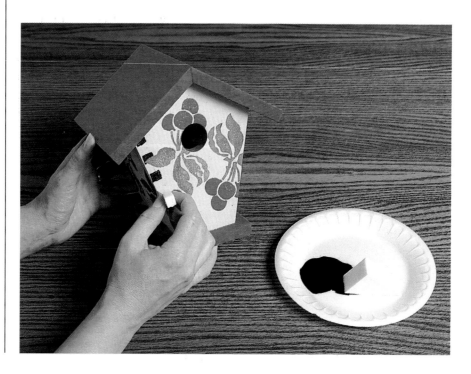

Project

Child-size unfinished
table and chairs

Foam Stamps

Decorative scroll
(61023)

Checkerboard (61010)

Abstract cut-paper
(63006)

Country folk art (64001)

Stamping Paints

*(For stamping the
project and
basecoating the table
legs)*

Lavender

Fuchsia

Blue jay

Crocus yellow

Seminole green

Miscellaneous

Fine sandpaper

Tack cloth

White latex paint, satin
finish *(for basecoating
the table and chairs)*

1-inch paintbrush

Scrap paper

Scissors

Wedge-shaped
applicator sponges and
paper or plastic plates
(for inking the stamps)

Ruler

Pencil

Rubber eraser *(to erase
pencil lines)*

Plastic eraser *(for the
square stamp)*

Synthetic-bristle
varnishing brush

Water-based
polyurethane,
semigloss finish

VARIATION: CHILDREN'S TABLE AND CHAIRS

The stamp images for this project were selected from a few foam stamp kits; some were cut apart to make stamping easier. You may prefer to use images from just one kit, or mix and match motifs from your own collection.

1. Sand the table and chairs until smooth. Wipe lightly with a tack cloth.

2. Apply two coats of white latex paint to the table and chairs. Let dry.

3. Stamp and cut out several paper patterns for each motif. Lay out the design on the chairs as shown. For the tabletop border, lay out the short sides with full checkerboard paper patterns, and the long sides with patterns that have been cut in half lengthwise. Use a ruler and a pencil to lightly mark the outer parameters of the tabletop border.

4. Remove the paper patterns one at a time and stamp the images on the table and chairs. Make sure to clean stamps thoroughly when changing colors. After the prints have dried, gently erase the pencil marks from the tabletop.

5. Stamp checkerboards in various colors on the chair and table aprons and on the backs and fronts of the chair rungs. Let dry.

6. Cut a square from a plastic eraser the same size as one of the squares in the checkerboard stamp. Stamp it in various colors around the perimeter of the tabletop and the chair seats and along the bottom edge of the top rung on each chair.

7. Paint each leg of the table in a different color. Let dry. Dip the tip of the paintbrush handle into the paint to add large and small polka dots in various colors to the table and chair legs. Reload the handle before making each dot. Let dry.

8. Apply two to three coats of polyurethane. Let dry between each coat.

"Swirling" Highboy

MATERIALS AND SUPPLIES

Project

Chest of drawers

Stamps

For the chest

Swirl foam stamp (Primitive collection, 63003)

For the drawer pulls

Swirl rubber stamp (Cut-paper art collection, 760.03)

Acrylics

(for basecoating)

Tomato spice

Black

Stamping Paints and Inks

Gold stamping paint *(for the chest)*

Black pigment ink *(for the clay)*

Polymer Clay

Gold: seven 2-ounce bars

Red golden: five 2-ounce bars

Miscellaneous

Commercial paint and varnish remover

Wood putty

Putty knife

Sandpaper

Tack cloth

Paintbrushes

Wedge-shaped applicator sponge and plastic or paper plate *(for inking the foam stamp)*

Wooden drawer knobs

Brass upholstery tacks

Water-based polyurethane, gloss finish

*T*ransform an outdated piece of furniture or a garage sale find into a one-of-a-kind conversation piece. For this project, an old chest of drawers was refinished in acrylic paints and stamped with golden swirls. The unusual drawer pulls were created by covering plain wooden knobs with polymer clay, which was then printed with rubber stamps and accented with brass upholstery tacks.

1. Remove all hardware. Strip off the existing finish with paint and varnish remover. Fill any holes or cracks with wood putty; let dry. Sand well, then wipe lightly with a tack cloth.

2. Apply two to three coats of tomato spice acrylic paint to the drawer fronts and the sides of the chest, letting each coat dry before adding the next. Paint the top of the chest and any remaining areas with black acrylic. Paint the knobs with black, then set aside. Let dry.

Before repainting, remove hardware, strip off the finish, and make any necessary repairs.

Paint the sides of the chest and the drawer fronts in red, and the rest in black.

3. Stamp each of the drawer fronts with the swirl foam stamp and gold stamping paint. If desired, use the photograph on page 89 as a guide to the placement of the prints. You may need to adjust the design to accommodate the proportions of your particular piece.

4. Condition 1 ounce of gold clay, then roll it into a ball. Press a drawer knob into the ball, flattening it until it molds around the knob's edges. (It may be necessary to roll the knob around to do this.) Make sure that the clay surface on the front of the knob is flat. Use the swirl rubber stamp to print an all-over pattern in the clay on the front of the knob. Repeat this step for the remaining knobs.

5. Divide 2 ounces of red golden clay into fourths. Condition each piece and roll it into a ball. Flatten the ball slightly, then press it firmly on top of the gold clay. Ink the swirl rubber stamp with black pigment ink, then stamp the red clay with a circular design. Press a brass upholstery tack into the center of the red clay. Repeat this step for the remaining knobs.

6. Cure the knobs in an oven following the label instructions on the clay; let cool. Seal the clay on the knobs with a coat of polyurethane. Let dry before screwing into the drawers.

Stamp the swirl foam stamp on the drawer fronts in gold.

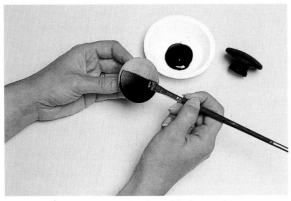

Paint the wooden drawer knobs in black. Let dry.

Flatten a ball of gold clay onto a drawer knob.

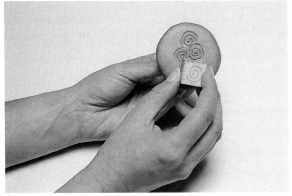

Impress the uninked swirl rubber stamp into the clay.

Flatten a ball of red clay and press it firmly onto the gold clay. Ink the rubber stamp with black pigment ink, then stamp the red clay. Finish with a brass upholstery tack.

Cure the clay as directed, let cool, then seal with a coat of polyurethane.

Mica Collage Table

MATERIALS AND SUPPLIES

Project

Unfinished console table with apron

Rubber Stamps

Giraffe (A825E)

Giraffe skin print (A853E)

Paints, Inks, and Embossing Powders

Black acrylic paint *(for basecoating the table)*

Black pigment ink *(for stamping)*

Transparent embossing powder

Pigment Powders

Copper

Russet red

Gold

Miscellaneous

Assorted natural-fiber art papers, including a black-and-gold checkerboard print paper

Embossing heat tool

Mica tiles

Perfect Paper Adhesive

Paintbrush

Metal ruler

Craft knife

*T*his unusual console table is a guaranteed conversation piece. Most of the tabletop is collaged with an assortment of art papers stamped with giraffes, while a narrow central panel is a collage of translucent mica leaves stamped with a giraffe skin print. Once available only at gem and geology stores, mica has recently been brought to light as a stamping surface and collage element, and can now be purchased at many art supply and craft stores.

The matching lampshade is fashioned from a sheet of beautiful handmade paper stamped with a giraffe, and features a cutout finished with a sheer leaf of stamped mica that lets the light shine through.

1. Paint the entire table with one coat of black acrylic. Let dry.
2. Stamp and emboss several art papers with the giraffe stamp using black pigment ink and clear embossing powder. Tear the paper around each print to create a deckle edge, then tear the other papers (except for the checkerboard print paper) into irregular shapes. Set aside.
3. Carefully separate the mica tiles into individual leaves.

Separate the mica tiles into leaves.

Susan Pickering Rothamel

4. Stamp the giraffe skin print pattern on one of the leaves with black pigment ink, then emboss it with clear embossing powder.

5. Place some Perfect Paper Adhesive on a paper or plastic plate, then mix it with a small amount of one of the powdered pigments. Apply the mixture to the embossed tile with a paintbrush. Let dry.

6. Repeat step 4 with the remaining leaves. Mix the two remaining colors of powdered pigment with some adhesive, then brush each embossed leaf with one of the three colors.

7. Mask off a narrow rectangular panel in the center of the tabletop with masking tape. Position the embossed leaves within the panel, leaving a small amount of space between them, then trim them with a ruler and craft knife so they fit precisely at the edges. Use some unmixed adhesive to glue the leaves down. Let dry, then remove the masking tape.

8. Layer and glue the torn art papers and giraffe prints on the rest of the tabletop, extending to its edge. Use plenty of adhesive to ensure that the papers are glued down firmly.

9. Cut the checkerboard print paper into long, thin strips with a ruler and craft knife. Paste down the strips to make a border around the central tabletop panel, and to embellish the apron and legs.

The completed tabletop.

Stamp the giraffe skin print pattern on a single leaf with black pigment ink, then emboss with clear embossing powder.

"Tiled" Storage Chest

MATERIALS AND SUPPLIES

Project

Small wood chest of drawers, either finished or unfinished

Rubber Stamps

(Use rubber stamps only; other types cannot withstand the heat of the melted powder)

Assorted images that fit the dimensions of the tiles

Inks

Clear embossing ink

Pigment inks in assorted colors (including black)

Embossing Powders

(Use a coarse-granulation embossing powder, such as Suze Weinberg's Ultra Thick Embossing Enamel)

Clear

Gold

Black

Interference blue

Other Media

Pigment powders, rub-on metallic pastes, and glitter glues in assorted colors

Miscellaneous

$1/8$-inch-thick cardboard

Craft knife

Metal ruler

Embossing heat tool

Strong adhesive (such as double-stick tape, silicone glue, or a glue gun)

Thin sheets of metal

Dull scissors *(for cutting the metal)*

Ball-tipped stylus

Drawer handles

*T*his project demonstrates a resourceful way to make lustrous, ceramic-look tiles out of plain cardboard. The entire surface of a rectangle of cardboard is coated first with embossing or pigment ink, then with a coarse-granulation embossing powder (referred to by various brand names, including Embossing Enamel), which is melted with an embossing heat tool. A glossy surface is established by repeating this step twice more. Then, while the final application of embossing powder is still hot, it is printed with a rubber stamp inked with pigment ink. Pigment powders, metallic pastes, and glitter glues in various colors are used to enhance and complement each stamp print.

Because the cardboard can be cut into any shape or size, the tiles can be used to adorn just about anything; make sure to measure the areas you want to cover before you begin. If you prefer to completely conceal a wood base, basecoating with either acrylic or latex paint is recommended.

1. Use a sharp craft knife and a metal ruler to cut the cardboard into $2^3/_8$-inch squares.
2. Apply embossing ink to the entire surface of one side of a cardboard square. Sprinkle with embossing powder, then melt with an embossing heat tool. Repeat twice more, starting with either embossing or pigment ink.

Apply embossing ink and coarse-grained embossing powder to a cardboard square, then melt with a heat tool. Repeat twice more.

3. Before melting the third application of embossing powder, ink one of the rubber stamps with pigment ink, then set aside. While the third application of embossing powder is still hot, impress it with the inked stamp. (The embossing powder solidifies instantly so that the stamp can be removed easily, and the ink acts as a protective lubricant for the rubber.)

4. For a metallic look, brush the embossed surface with powdered pigment. To intensify the metallic sheen, rub on some metallic paste or glitter glue.

5. Repeat steps 2 through 4 on the remaining cardboard squares, using various combinations of stamp images and media to achieve a range of effects.

6. Apply black pigment ink to the face of each drawer, then sprinkle with gold embossing powder and heat with the embossing tool. Use your finger to apply several colors of powdered pigment to each drawer front.

7. Attach the cardboard tiles to the sides and top of the chest with a strong adhesive (see the materials list on page 96 for suggestions).

8. Measure the areas surrounding the drawers and the edges on the top and sides of the chest. Cut the metal as needed, then affix the pieces to the chest with strong adhesive. Texturize the metal strips by striking them carefully with a ball-tipped stylus. Attach the handles to the drawer fronts.

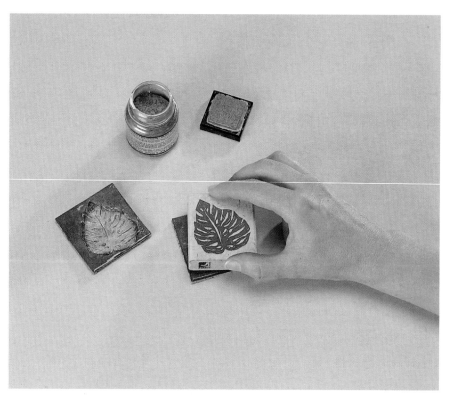

Before melting the third application, ink a rubber stamp with pigment ink, then set aside. While the embossing powder is still hot, impress it with the inked stamp.

Brush the surface of the "tile" with powdered pigment.

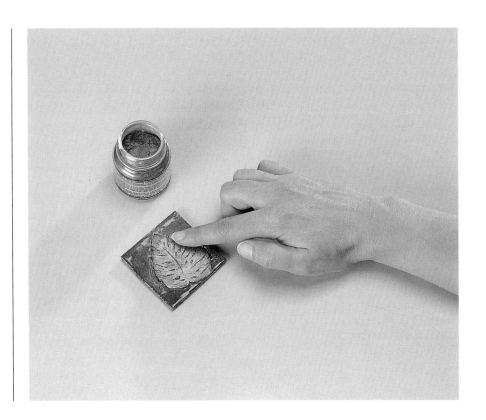

The completed chest top.

Heart Bed Linens

MATERIALS AND SUPPLIES

Project

White sheet set with two pillowcases

Patterns

See below *(use at same size)*

Stamp Supplies

Tracing paper

Pencil

Graphite paper OR carbon paper

Linoleum block, printing block, OR large eraser

Assorted carving tools (including a V-tool)

Craft knife

Stamping Paints

Medium red

Miscellaneous

Scrap paper and scissors *(for making the paper patterns)*

Several sheets of blank newsprint *(to prevent bleed-through on the pillowcases)*

Wedge-shaped applicator sponges and paper or plastic plate *(for inking the stamps)*

By using stamps you've carved yourself, you can create charming bed linens by printing a simple design on plain white sheets. To revitalize your bedroom decor, paint the walls with the same color you use to stamp the sheets, then stamp a wall border in white using the same motifs.

1. Wash and dry the sheet set according to label instructions. If needed, press the cases and top sheet lightly to straighten the fabric grain. Set the fitted or bottom sheet aside.
2. Trace the patterns below using tracing paper and a pencil. Transfer the traced patterns to the block or eraser by placing a sheet of carbon or graphite paper on it, carbon or graphite side down, positioning the tracing over it, then retracing the patterns with a pencil.

3. Carve along the outlines of each motif with a V-tool. Use the other tools to remove areas of the block or eraser that you *don't* want to print. Trim around both motifs with a craft knife.

4. Make several paper patterns of each image, either by stamping them several times on scrap paper or by making several photocopies of a single print.

5. Spread the pillowcases on your work surface, cut out the patterns, then lay them out as desired. In the design shown below, four hearts were arranged so that the tip of each is oriented toward a central point, then flourishes were added at the point where their curves meet. Flourishes were also positioned at regular intervals along each case's border. The center flourish was placed first, then the two at either end; once their positions were established, the remaining images could be arranged accurately.

After carving the stamps, make several paper patterns of each image, then use them to determine your layout.

6. Insert a few sheets of blank newsprint into each pillowcase. Use a wedge-shaped applicator sponge to ink the heart stamp with red paint. Leaving the flourish patterns in place, remove each heart pattern immediately before stamping its print. (Do *not* discard the patterns; set them aside so they can be used again in step 7.) Once all the hearts have been stamped and allowed to dry, repeat this step with the flourish stamp. Let dry.

7. Arrange the top sheet on your work surface. Reusing the paper patterns, repeat steps 5 and 6 on the top sheet. Alternating hearts and flourishes, stamp the border so that the prints face right side up when the sheet is folded over.

8. Heat-set the stamp prints on the pillowcases and the top sheet according to the fabric ink manufacturer's instructions.

Leave all the patterns in place until you are ready to stamp, then remove each one just before stamping its print.

Overprinted Floral Placemat

*U*sing simple potato and eraser stamp
images, white sheeting can serve as the
backdrop for colorful placemats. The solid
colors were printed first with a broad-surface
potato stamp, then the details were overprinted
slightly off-center with a carved linoleum
stamp to give the pattern a charming,
handmade look.

MATERIALS AND SUPPLIES

Patterns

Page 155

Project

For one placemat

(includes 1/2-inch seam allowance)

Two 20- × 14-inch rectangles of white sheeting

One 20- × 14-inch rectangle of cotton batting

White thread

Stamp Supplies

For the linoleum stamp

Tracing paper

Pencil

Linoleum block

Graphite paper OR carbon paper

Carving tools

Craft knife

For the potato stamp

Paring knife

Potatoes

Craft knife

Stamping Paints

Fuchsia

Seminole green

Black

Miscellaneous

Scrap paper

Scissors

Disappearing ink fabric marker

Small paintbrush

Wedge-shaped applicator sponges and paper or
plastic plates *(for inking the stamps)*

Black textile marker

1. Wash and dry the sheeting as per the label instructions. If necessary, iron it to straighten the grain.
2. Trace the rose and leaf pattern on page 155 using tracing paper and a pencil.
3. To transfer the traced patterns to the linoleum block, place a sheet of carbon or graphite paper on the block, carbon or graphite side down, position the tracing over it, then retrace the patterns with a pencil. Use the carving tools to remove areas of the linoleum that you *don't* want to print. Trim around both images with the craft knife.
4. Stamp the linoleum images on a piece of scrap paper and cut them out.
5. Slice a potato in half. Place one scrap paper pattern printed side down on each potato half. Trace the outline of each pattern with the craft knife, then remove the areas of the potato that fall outside the outlines.
6. On the right side of one piece of sheeting, use the disappearing ink fabric marker to make a border approximately 3 inches from the edge.
7. Ink the potato rose stamp by brushing fuchsia paint on its carved surface. Using the fabric marker border as a guideline, stamp the sheeting. Re-ink the potato after making each print. Let dry.
8. Repeat step 7 with the potato leaf stamp, applying the green paint to its surface with a wedge sponge. Let dry.
9. Ink the linoleum rose stamp with black paint using the flat edge of a wedge sponge, then overprint the potato rose prints slighty off-center. Repeat with the linoleum leaf stamp to overprint the potato leaf prints.
10. Clean the linoleum leaf stamp and apply green paint with the wedge sponge. Stamp several prints around the border. Use the black textile marker to draw a squiggly line over the disappearing ink border. Let dry, then heat-set the inks according to the manufacturer's instructions.
11. With the right sides of the sheeting together and the batting on the bottom, sew all four sides of the placemat, leaving a 6-inch opening on one side. Trim the seams, clip the corners, turn the placemat right side out, then slipstitch the opening closed.

Use carving tools and a craft knife to remove the linoleum between the traced areas.

Make paper patterns of the linoleum stamps.

Use the patterns as templates for cutting the potato stamps.

Ink and print the potato rose stamp in fuchsia.

Repeat with the potato leaf stamp in green.

Overprint the potato prints with the linoleum stamps in black.

Fruit Harvest Floorcloth

Available in a wide range of shapes and sizes, canvas floorcloth "blanks" are typically found at stores that carry art, craft, and sewing supplies. If the assortment of ready-mades doesn't meet your needs, you can buy canvas yardage, either raw (unprimed) or pre-gessoed (already primed), at fabric and art supply stores. Instructions for working with raw canvas yardage and for hemming a finished floorcloth are also included.

The floorcloth was basecoated with acrylics, but latex paints can also be used. To make the prints, stamping paints were applied directly to the foam stamp dies, and blended for the pears and foliage. The colors of the pears and grapes not only evoke the autumn harvest, but comprise a beautiful analogous color scheme. The shadows and vine tendrils, which were painted freehand, add visual interest.

MATERIALS AND SUPPLIES

Project

29- × 40-inch canvas floorcloth blank OR a 30- × 41-inch piece of canvas yardage, selvages removed

Foam Stamps

Pear and grape (from kit 63008)

Acrylic Paints

For basecoating

Butter yellow

Wedgewood green

Stamping Paints

Yellow

Bright red

Hunter green

Kelly green

Eggplant

Hippo gray

Autumn brown

Miscellaneous

Acrylic gesso, extra-fine sandpaper, and tack cloth *(optional, for raw canvas)*

Chalk pencil *(optional, for canvas yardage)*

Masking tape

Paintbrushes in assorted sizes (from 2 inches wide to a lettering brush)

Wedge-shaped applicator sponges and paper or plastic plates *(for inking the stamps)*

Scissors, fabric glue, and rolling pin *(optional, for hemming canvas yardage)*

Synthetic-bristle varnishing brush

Water-based polyurethane, satin finish

1. If you're working with a canvas blank, proceed to step 2. If you're working with pre-gessoed canvas, lightly mark a 1-inch hem around the perimeter of the front with a chalk pencil. If you're working with raw canvas, apply two coats of acrylic gesso to the front, letting the first dry before applying the second. Once the second coat is dry, sand it lightly, then wipe it with a tack cloth. Use a chalk pencil to mark a 1-inch hem on the front.
2. Mask off a 21½- × 31¼-inch panel in the center of the canvas. Paint the panel with yellow acrylic paint. Let dry, then remove the tape.
3. Mask off the edges of the center panel, then paint the border with green acrylic. Let dry, then remove the tape.
4. To ink the pear stamp, pour a little each of the yellow, red, and green stamping paints on a plate. Using a separate wedge sponge for each color, apply yellow paint to the pear portion of the die, then shade by applying red to its edges. Ink the foliage by applying the lighter green first, then shading with the darker green. Re-ink the stamp after making each print. Let dry.

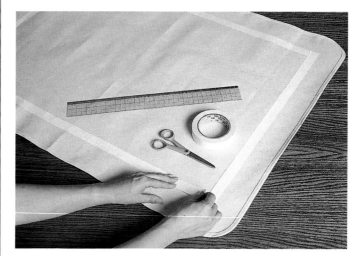

Mask off a panel in the center of the canvas, paint in yellow, let dry, then remove the tape.

Mask the edges of the yellow center panel, then paint the border in green. Once dry, remove the tape.

5. For the grapes stamp, ink the grape cluster with eggplant paint, then blend the two greens on the foliage. Re-ink the stamp after making each print. Let dry.
6. To print an individual grape leaf, clean the entire stamp thoroughly, blend the two greens on the foliage, then stamp the floorcloth. Repeat as desired. Let dry.
7. Blend the brown and gray paints, then use a brush to paint tendrils. Thin down some gray paint with water, then shade the fruit by painting a thin band along one side. Let dry. To finish a canvas blank, proceed to step 9. For hemming instructions, see step 8.
8. Crease the hem, fold it to the back of the cloth, then miter the corners to prevent the edges from curling up. Working on one side at a time, apply glue to the wrong side of the canvas, then use a rolling pin to eliminate creases and air bubbles. Weight the corners and let dry overnight before applying polyurethane.
9. Apply four coats of polyurethane. Let dry between coats.

Blend the colors for the pears and its leaves directly on the die. Repeat for the foliage on the grapes stamp.

Paint the tendrils and shadows freehand.

Stamped Ribbon Pillows

MATERIALS AND SUPPLIES

100-Percent Cotton Ribbon

Includes ¹/₂-inch seam allowance

For the striped pillow

Five 10-inch lengths of 1¹/₂-inch-wide cream ribbon

Six 10-inch lengths of 1¹/₂-inch-wide sage ribbon

For the woven pillow

Seven 10¹/₂-inch lengths of 1¹/₂-inch-wide cream ribbon

Seven 10¹/₂-inch lengths of 1¹/₂-inch-wide purple ribbon

Rubber Stamps

For the striped pillow

Small flower and leaf (Posh gallery set, 761.01)

For the woven pillow

Flower stamp (Japanese collage kit, 977.03)

Fabric Ink Pads

Fuchsia

Emerald green

Sewing Supplies

Fusible webbing

Scissors

Iron

Solid-color fabrics *(for the pillow backings)*

Needle and thread

Polyester fiberfill

Fabric glue

Flat-backed pearls

Miscellaneous

Pencil OR chopstick *(for turning out the corners of the stitched pillow)*

*R*ibbon offers a quick and easy way to make a stamped fabric project without having to do a lot of sewing. To make these pillows, two contrasting colors of cotton ribbon were arranged in simple patterns, stamped, then ironed to fusible webbing, which bonds to fabric without stitching. Pieces of fabric in complementary or contrasting colors were used to finish off the backs of the pillows, and flat-backed pearls glued to the centers of the stamped flowers add textural interest. The applications for stamped ribbons aren't restricted to pillows. They can also be used to decorate paper gift boxes, to embellish a variety of table linens, or to trim clothing and personal accessories.

Because they are preshrunk and accept fabric ink well, cotton and cotton-blend ribbons are best suited to stamping. Note that some fabric inks may bleed on satin and polyester ribbon, so run tests on small scraps before stamping an entire purchase.

STRIPED PILLOW

The finished dimensions of this pillow are 9¹/₂ × 16 inches.

1. Arrange the ribbons in alternating stripes of cream and sage.
2. Stamp three flower prints in fuchsia ink along each length of cream ribbon, leaving an equal amount of space between the prints. On each length of sage ribbon, stamp two flower prints in fuchsia ink, centering them vertically within the spaces between prints on the adjoining cream ribbons. Let dry.

On the cream ribbons, stamp three flower prints in fuchsia, leaving an equal amount of space between them. On the sage ribbons, stamp two flower prints in fuchsia, centering them vertically within the spaces between prints on the adjoining cream ribbons.

3. To each flower print, add three leaf prints in green ink. If desired, position the prints so that the foliage is the same within each ribbon color. Let dry.

4. Cut a piece of fusible webbing to 10 × 16½ inches. Peel off the release paper, then arrange the stamped ribbons over the fusible webbing. To fuse the ribbons to the webbing, fill an iron with water, then preheat it on the "cotton" setting. Working a small area at a time, press firmly with the iron while applying steam continuously.

5. Cut a rectangle of solid-color fabric to the same dimensions as the fused ribbons. Place the fabric and ribbon right sides together. Using a ½-inch seam allowance, sew all four sides, leaving a 6-inch opening. Clip the corners, trim the seams, and turn the pillow inside out. (If necessary, use the eraser end of a pencil or a chopstick to turn corners out.) Stuff the pillow with fiberfill, then slipstitch the opening closed. Glue a pearl to the center of each flower.

Add three leaf prints in green to each flower print.

Bond the ribbons to the fusible webbing with a hot steam iron.

WOVEN PILLOW

This completed pillow measures 10 inches square.

1. Cut a 10½-inch square of fusible webbing. Peel off the release paper, then arrange the lengths of cream ribbon over it horizontally. Carefully interweave lengths of purple ribbon with the cream ribbon.

2. Stamp each of the three cream squares in rows 2, 4, and 6 with a flower print in fuchsia ink. Clean the stamp well, then stamp each of the two innermost cream squares in rows 3 and 5 with a flower print in green ink. Let dry.

3. Fuse the ribbon to the webbing as noted on the opposite page in step 4, then assemble and finish the pillow as noted in step 5.

Arrange the cream ribbon over the fusible webbing.

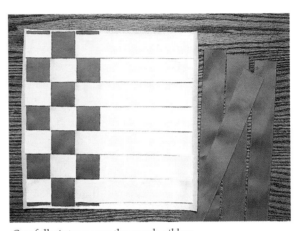

Carefully interweave the purple ribbon.

Stamp each of the three cream squares in rows 2, 4, and 6 with a fuchsia flower print, then stamp each of the two innermost cream squares in rows 3 and 5 with a green print.

Cottage Rose Curtains and Valance

MATERIALS AND SUPPLIES

Project

See "Measuring Your Windows" for yardage and cutting guidelines

Cream-colored muslin

Foam Stamps

Corner rose and single rose (Wallpaper roses kit, 63007)

Stamping Paints

Dusty rose

Lavender

Wedgewood green

Hunter green

Sewing Supplies

Ruler

Thread

Scissors

Fade-away fabric marker *(optional, if marking a grid for a repeat pattern)*

Miscellaneous

Blank newsprint

Wedge-shaped applicator sponges and paper or plastic plate *(for inking the stamps)*

Scrap paper, scissors, and low-tack masking tape *(for the paper patterns)*

Create charming curtains that call to mind a cottage hideaway by stamping cream-colored muslin with stencil-look roses. Versatile enough to complement virtually any decor, muslin is a classic choice for fabric stamping.

MEASURING YOUR WINDOWS

The finished measurements of the valance and curtains shown on the opposite page are as follows:

- *Valance.* 85 inches wide (with a 1-inch double hem on either side); $20^1/_2$ inches long at the longest point, $15^1/_2$ at the shortest.
- *Side panels.* Each 40 inches wide (with a 1-inch double hem on either side) by 80 inches long (with a 2-inch double bottom hem).

The dimensions of your windows will dictate the length and width of both the side panels and the valance. The length of the valance must balance with the proportions of the window and remain in keeping with the scale of the rest of the room. Also, its casing must be wide enough to accommodate the valance hardware. (Ours was 4 inches wide.) For the side panels, add enough yardage to make two 1-inch double side hems, a 2-inch double bottom hem, and a casing large enough to accommodate the width of your curtain rod.

VALANCE

1. In this project, the size and shape of the corner stamp guided the design of the valance. Each triangle measures $8^1/_2$ inches wide at its base. Measure the overall width and length you'll need, then cut two pieces for the valance. With right sides together, mark and cut the triangle-edge finish along the bottom, placing the point of a triangle at the center of the fabric width.
2. Set one piece of the valance aside. Protect your work surface with sheets of blank newsprint, then place the other piece of the valance over it. Using a separate wedge sponge for each color, ink the die of the corner stamp directly, applying dusty mauve to the rose, lavender to the ribbon, and a blend of the two greens to the foliage. On the right side of the fabric, stamp the corner rose, aligning the print with the point of a triangle. Re-ink the stamp before making each print.

3. Let the prints dry thoroughly, then heat-set the paints following the manufacturer's instructions.

4. Place the two pieces of the valance right sides together. Using a $1/4$-inch seam allowance, stitch along the entire length of the triangular edge, then cut a small slit into each of the corners and trim the points. Stitch the sides of the valance, again using a $1/4$-inch seam allowance.

5. Turn the valance inside out and press flat. Press each side of the valance to make 1-inch double hems. Machine-stitch the hems, then press.

6. Machine-stitch a casing along the top of the valance. Press well.

SIDE PANELS

1. Measure and cut the fabric you'll need for each panel.

2. On each panel, press a 1-inch double hem on either side and a 2-inch double hem at the bottom. Machine-stitch in place.

3. At the top of each panel, press a casing large enough to accommodate the curtain rod.

4. Make several prints of the single rose stamp on scrap paper, then cut them out and affix a loop of low-tack masking tape to the back of each. Working on one panel at a time and starting slightly above the bottom hem, place a pattern at the center of the panel and one on either end. Using these as guides, continue to position patterns on the panel, adjusting the arrangement until you are pleased with the spacing. In this project, the panels feature a tossed half-drop repeat. For a less structured appearance, remove each pattern just prior to stamping. For a more precise look, make sure the spacing between motifs is consistent, then follow the instructions on page 77 for marking a grid for a repeat pattern.

5. Cover your work surface with sheets of blank newsprint. Position the panel over the newsprint, then stamp its entire length. Using a separate wedge sponge for each color, ink the stamp die directly, applying dusty mauve to the rose and a blend of the two greens to the foliage. Re-ink the stamp before making each print.

6. Repeat steps 4 and 5 on the remaining panels. Let the prints dry, then heat-set the paints according to the manufacturer's instructions. Machine-stitch the casings to finish.

Align the point of each stamp print with the point of one of the valance's triangles.

Use paper patterns to determine the arrangement of images on your panels. This panel has been stamped with a tossed layout (the roses are oriented in several different directions) in a half-drop repeat.

"Embossed" Velvet Throw

MATERIALS AND SUPPLIES

Project

Includes ¹/₂-inch seam allowance

One 43-inch square of velvet (plus some extra for making practice prints)

One 43-inch square of satin

Rubber Stamp

Large butterfly OR other large broad-surface motif

Other Sewing Supplies

Chalk *(optional, if marking the positions of the prints on the velvet)*

Thread

5 yards of gold fringe

Pins

Velvet Embossing Supplies

Water in a fine-mist spray bottle

Iron

Bond-weight scrap paper

Craft knife

Miscellaneous

Scrap paper, scissors, and low-tack masking tape *(optional, for making the paper patterns)*

---

*T*his throw, which was "embossed" without using ink, paint, or embossing powder, can add a touch of elegance to any room. Featuring large, randomly placed butterflies, it can be arranged casually on a sofa as a striking color accent, or draped over a sideboard to create a romantic dinner vignette. The finished throw shown opposite measures 42 inches square (excluding the fringe).

Note that only rubber stamps can withstand the heat of the iron that is integral to this technique. Broad-surface images with few details give the best results. When laundering the velvet, follow the manufacturer's instructions. In my experience, neither washing nor dry-cleaning will remove embossed prints.

1. Before attempting to emboss the throw, experiment on one or two scrap pieces of the velvet. Drain the water from the iron, then preheat it on the permanent press setting. Place the stamp die side up on a hard, flat surface.
2. Position a piece of velvet nap side down over the die. Lightly mist the area of the velvet over the die with water. Place a sheet of paper over the iron's steam vents, then apply the iron to the dampened velvet for about 20 seconds.

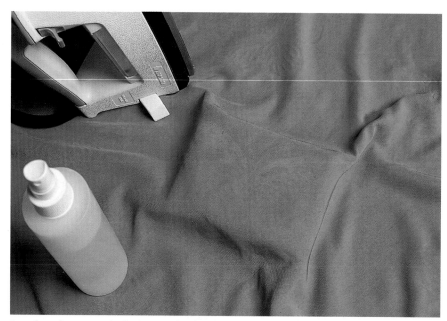

Lay the velvet nap side down over the die, which is positioned right side up, then lightly mist the area with water before applying the iron.

3. Turn the velvet over and evaluate your test print. If the area of the die surrounding the image has also been impressed into the nap, carefully cut it away with a craft knife before making another print.

4. Once you've made a successful test print, place the large square of velvet for the throw nap side down on your work surface. If desired, mark the positions of your prints on the back of the fabric with chalk. (Paper patterns can also be used; see pages 53 and 76.) Repeat step 2 over the entire surface of the fabric.

5. Place the embossed velvet and the satin right sides together. Position the fringe between the two fabrics so that its woven edge is aligned with their edges and its tassels are enclosed between them. Pin in place, then machine-stitch on all four sides, leaving a 6-inch opening. Clip the corners, turn right side out, then slipstitch the opening closed.

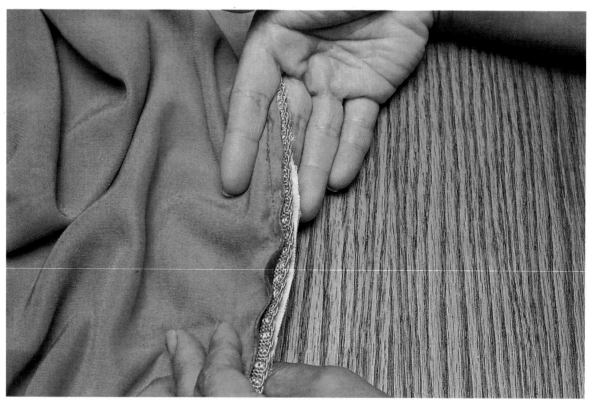

To make the throw, place the velvet and the satin right sides together, insert the fringe between them, pin in place, then machine-stitch its entire perimeter, leaving a 6-inch opening. Turn the throw inside out, then finish the stitching by hand.

Engineered Lemon Wall Vine

MATERIALS AND SUPPLIES

Foam Stamp

Lemon (Fruit kit, 63008)

Stamping Paints

Bright yellow

Terracotta

Seminole green

Hunter green

Miscellaneous

Mild soap, water, and sponge *(optional, for cleaning the wall)*

Latex paint *(optional, for refreshing the wall surface)*

Scrap paper, scissors, and low-tack masking tape *(for making the paper patterns)*

Wedge-shaped applicator sponges and paper or plastic plates *(for inking the stamps)*

Small round brush *(for handpainting the branches and other details)*

A somewhat unusual choice for a kitchen fixture, the sconce-style cement planter in the breakfast nook of my new home was installed in such a way that removing it would have made repairing the wall a major undertaking. Instead, I decided to soften its appearance and make it consistent with the rest of the decor by stamping an engineered design in a loose, informal style. The meandering vine of cheerful yellow lemons brings light and warmth to a once dreary corner.

123

1. To prepare the wall for stamping, either clean it with a mild soap-and-water solution and wipe it down with a damp sponge, or refresh it with a coat or two of latex paint. (If desired, a layer of translucent glaze or another faux finish can also be applied.)

2. Ink and stamp just the lemon portion of the stamp several times on scrap paper, then cut the prints out. Affix a loop of masking tape to the back of each paper pattern, then position the patterns on the wall to determine the arrangement. In this project, the lemons were placed somewhat randomly.

3. Using a separate wedge sponge for each color, ink only the lemon portion of the stamp with yellow paint, then softly blend terracotta to add dimension. Remove one of the paper patterns, then stamp a print in its place. Repeat this step for the remaining lemon patterns. Use the round brush and the terracotta paint to add a small stem at the top of each lemon. Let dry.

4. Clean the stamp well. Again using a separate wedge sponge for each color, ink the foliage portion of the stamp by blending the two greens on the die, then stamp a print on the wall. Re-ink the stamp before making each print, varying the colors to suggest depth and dimension. (Dark green foliage will appear to advance, as if in the foreground, while light green foliage will appear as a "background" element.) Let dry.

5. When you've finished stamping leaves, step back and evaluate your composition. If necessary, stamp additional lemons and/or leaves to create a balanced distribution of motifs. Let dry.

6. If desired, use the round brush to extend the stems and add veins to the leaves.

After establishing a design with paper patterns, stamp the lemon prints, then paint a small stem at the top of each one.

Gold Fleur-de-Lis Wall

MATERIALS AND SUPPLIES

Foam Stamp
Small fleur-de-lis (Fleur-de-lis kit, 62005)

Stamping Paint
Gold

Miscellaneous
Mild soap, water, and sponge *(optional, for cleaning the wall)*

Latex paint *(optional, for refreshing the wall surface)*

Scrap paper, scissors, and low-tack masking tape *(for making the paper patterns)*

Wedge-shaped applicator sponge and paper or plastic plate *(for inking the stamp)*

Ruler

Plumb line

Pencil OR chalk

Cardboard and craft knife

T his dining room posed some significant decorating challenges: In addition to its small size, it has virtually no distinctive architectural features. The one outstanding visual element among the furnishings was the gold-leafed frames on the prints and mirrors. The solution: A small fleur-de-lis stamp, printed in metallic gold in a widely spaced, all-over half-drop layout, which accented the frames without overpowering the space or its contents.

1. Prepare the wall for stamping, either by cleaning it with a mild soap-and-water solution and wiping it down with a damp sponge, or by repainting it with latex paint. (If desired, a layer of translucent glaze or another faux finish can also be applied.)

2. Make several paper patterns of the image, either by stamping it several times on scrap paper or by making several photocopies of a single print. Cut the prints out, affix a loop of low-tack masking to the back of each one, then stick them to the center of the dominant wall to determine spacing and position. It isn't necessary to cover the entire wall, just enough of it to give you a general idea. When you are pleased with the layout, adjust the spacing to devise a consistent repeat.

3. Ask someone to help you hang a plumb line from the ceiling at or near the center of the dominant wall over a vertical arrangement of motifs. Remove each paper pattern, very lightly marking its center point in pencil or chalk. Measure the distances from the center point of one motif to those surrounding it, then use these measurements to cut a rectangle from the cardboard.

Hang a plumb line from the ceiling to establish a vertical guideline at or near the center of the dominant wall.

4. This project features a half-drop repeat, so the cardboard rectangle should be positioned so that the plumb line intersects its top and bottom points, which should each be touching the center point of a motif. Use pencil or chalk to lightly mark all four corners of the cardboard. Repeat, first along the entire length of the plumb line, then moving out on either side to mark the entire wall.

5. Use the applicator sponge to ink the stamp with gold paint. Gently erase a pencil mark or dust off a chalk mark, then stamp the image. Repeat, re-inking the stamp and removing the mark on the wall right before making each print. It may be helpful to establish a rhythm by stamping from left to right and from top to bottom until the entire wall is complete. Let dry.

6. If desired, repeat step 5 for the remaining walls. Let dry.

To mark a grid for a half-drop repeat, align the premeasured cardboard rectangle so that the vertical guideline intersects two of its corners.

Fleur-de-Lis Collage Mat

MATERIALS AND SUPPLIES

Project

16- × 20-inch white mat board frame

Foam Stamps

Large and small fleurs-de-lis (62005 and 61005)

Stamping Paints

Tomato spice

Eggplant

Metallic gold

Collage Supplies

Black-and-white photocopies of handwritten script and old documents

Plain white bond-weight paper

Collage medium OR Perfect Paper Adhesive

Miscellaneous

Antiquing medium

Four small plastic containers *(for the diluted paints and antiquing medium)*

Scrap paper *(for protecting the work surface)*

Small flat synthetic-bristle paintbrush *(for painting the papers and applying collage medium)*

Wedge-shaped applicator sponges and paper or plastic plate *(for inking the stamps)*

Glass or plastic container *(for water, in which to rinse the paintbrush)*

*U*se an inexpensive picture mat as the foundation for a collage of an assortment of stamped papers. The collage papers, some of which feature beautiful examples of calligraphy and oldstyle typefaces, were painted with light washes of color, stamped with fleur-di-lis prints, and torn into uneven shapes before being layered and glued to the surface of the mat.

1. Pour a little of the antiquing medium and each color of stamping paint into a separate plastic mixing container. Dilute each paint with water until it reaches the translucent, watery consistency of traditional watercolor paints. Depending on the brand of antiquing medium you use, it may not be necessary to dilute it with water.

2. Cover your work surface with scrap paper. Paint the photocopies and plain white paper with the antiquing medium and diluted paints. Don't worry if your brushwork looks uneven; this effect will enhance the final look of the project.

Paint the plain papers and photocopies with washes of diluted stamping paint and antiquing medium.

3. Let dry. Clean the paintbrush so that it can be used later to apply collage medium (see step 7).

4. Pour a small amount of each color of stamping paint on a paper or plastic plate. Using a separate wedge sponge for each color, ink and print the two fleurs-de-lis on the colorwashed papers. Wash and dry the stamps thoroughly when changing paint colors. Let dry.

5. Tear the paper around each print into a jagged rectangle, or into a shape that follows the contours of each fleurs-de-lis.

Stamp the papers with fleur-de-lis prints in various colors, then tear into jagged shapes.

6. Place the prints on the mat, rearranging their position until you are happy with the design. Try layering smaller shapes over larger ones, and printed papers over plain. Be sure to maintain a good balance of colors in your layout.

7. Apply collage medium to the backs of the shapes with the flat paintbrush. Affix each shape to the mat, wrapping the edges of the larger pieces around the sides. Apply a coat of collage medium to the surface of the squares, smoothing out any air bubbles as you work. Let dry.

8. If desired, protect your work with a second coat of collage medium. Let dry.

Arrange the prints on the mat, then glue into place.

133

Papier-Mâché Bowl

I love the idea of creating something entirely
from scrap paper! This colorful bowl is made
by layering deep purple tissue paper over an
underlying newspaper shape, then pasting on
vibrant handmade art papers stamped with leaf
prints in vivid colors, which provide maximum
contrast against the dark background. A high-
gloss finish simultaneously heightens the colors
and protects the bowl's surface.

Once the papier-mâché form is complete,
the bowl itself can feature any number of
color combinations and motifs. For example,
handmade papers in earth tones can be paired
with nature-inspired stamps, and brightly
colored papers can serve as the background
for fun fruit prints.

MATERIALS AND SUPPLIES

Foam Stamp

Abstract leaf (61006)

Stamping Paints

Seminole green

Yellow

Papier-Mâché Supplies

Shallow bowl *(to serve as a mold)*

Plastic wrap

Newspaper

Wallpaper paste

Small flat synthetic-bristle paintbrush

Purple tissue paper

Yellow art paper

Red art paper

Miscellaneous

Wedge-shaped applicator sponges and plastic or
paper plate *(for inking the stamps)*

Water-based polyurethane, high-gloss finish

1. Cover the underside of the bowl with a layer of plastic wrap, stretching it tightly and taking care not to leave any gaps.

2. Tear the newspaper into small pieces. Apply wallpaper paste with a paintbrush to adhere the pieces to the underside of the bowl. Overlap the pieces, brushing them liberally with the paste. Continue until the entire surface of bowl has been covered with three to four layers of paper. Make sure that each layer is smooth and contains no air bubbles. Let dry thoroughly.

3. Repeat step 2 until the underside of the bowl is covered with a total of six to eight layers of paper. Let dry completely. (This may require several days.) Ease the papier-mâché bowl from the mold.

4. Tear the purple tissue paper into small pieces, arrange them in a single layer over the interior of the papier-mâché bowl, then brush them with wallpaper paste. Repeat to adhere another two layers.

5. Repeat step 4 on the underside of the bowl. Let dry.

6. Stamp six leaves in green on yellow paper. Clean the stamp, then stamp six leaves in yellow on red paper. Let the prints dry, then tear the paper around each print so that it follows its general contour.

7. Paste the yellow prints to the bowl, arranging them so that they all point toward its center. Tear a small circle of purple tissue, then glue it in the center. Paste the green leaves around rim of bowl, then place small torn pieces of red paper between them. Let dry completely.

8. Apply a coat of polyurethane to the interior of the bowl. Let dry. Repeat on the underside of the bowl.

Tightly wrap the underside of the mold with plastic wrap. Working a layer at a time, adhere small pieces of newspaper with wallpaper paste. Repeat until a total of six to eight layers have been pasted on the mold.

Once the bowl has dried completely, remove it from the mold. Arrange small pieces of purple tissue paper in a single layer over the interior, then brush with paste. Repeat to add two more layers to the interior, then repeat on the underside. Let dry.

Stamp the art papers with leaf prints in green and yellow, let dry, then tear to follow their outline.

Paste the leaf shapes to the interior of the bowl. Let dry.

Finish the completed bowl with a coat of polyurethane.

Orchard Mini-Chest

Printed with an assortment of fruit stamps rendered in a style reminiscent of Victorian illustrations, this charming chest of drawers is ideal for countertop storage in the kitchen but can easily be adapted for other rooms and uses. Stamped with flowers and vegetables, the chest could be used to store seed packets and twine; a container for small toys can be stamped with a child's favorite cartoon characters.

MATERIALS AND SUPPLIES

Project

Small unfinished wood chest

Rubber Stamps

Apple branch (A1582H)

Pear branch (A1583H)

Peach branch (A1584H)

Strawberries (A1585H)

Plum branch (A1586H)

Cherry branch (A1587H)

Fabric or Crafter's Ink

Black

Stamping Paints

Terracotta

Tomato spice

Yellow

Eggplant

Seminole green

Miscellaneous

Sandpaper

Tack cloth

Ivory acrylic paint

Antiquing medium

Wedge-shaped applicator sponges

Blue painter's tape

Small flat synthetic-bristle paintbrush *(for applying the acrylic paint, stamping paints, and polyurethane)*

Small plastic containers *(for the diluted paints)*

Pencil

Black permanent marker

Water-based polyurethane, matte finish

les poires

les pommes

les plumes

1. Remove the drawers from the chest. Sand all surfaces in the direction of the wood grain until smooth. Wipe lightly with a tack cloth to remove all sanding dust.

2. Basecoat all surfaces with ivory acrylic paint. Let dry. To create a distressed look, apply antiquing medium with the flat edge of a wedge sponge to the drawer fronts and top and sides of the chest.

3. Use the painter's tape to mask a 1/4-inch-wide border at the top and bottom edges of the drawer fronts. Paint with terracotta stamping paint, let dry, then carefully remove the tape. Repeat for the side edges of drawer fronts.

4. About 1/4 inch from the edges of the chest, mask a 1/4-inch border on its top and sides. Paint in terracotta, let dry, then remove the tape.

5. Mask all of the painted borders with lengths of painter's tape. Using a different fruit for each drawer front, randomly stamp prints in black fabric or crafter's ink. (When stamping the chest shown on pages 138–139, particular attention was paid as to how the colors of the fruits would complement each other once the drawers were in place.) Stamp a single print of three different fruits on either side, and one of every fruit on the top. Re-ink the stamps after making each print. Let dry, then remove the tape.

6. Place a little of each color of stamping paint into a separate plastic container, dilute with water until translucent, then use to color in the prints. Colors can be mixed as needed or desired to shade foliage and fruit. Let dry.

7. On the sides of the chest, write the names of each of the fruits in French, first in pencil (so that size and position can be adjusted, and errors can be erased), then with a black marker. Let dry.

8. Apply two to three coats of polyurethane to all visible surfaces. Let each coat dry before applying the next.

Basecoat the chest and drawers with ivory acrylic paint. Let dry, then sponge on antiquing medium.

Use painter's tape to mask narrow borders around the drawer fronts and on the top and sides of the chest, then paint with terracotta stamping paint. Let dry.

Mask the borders, then stamp the fruit prints.

Color the prints with thinned stamping paints.

Terracotta and Polymer Clay Pots

MATERIALS AND SUPPLIES

Project

Terracotta flower pots

Rubber Stamp

Falling leaves (Z720F)

Acrylic Paints

Tomato spice

Eggplant

Metallic gold

Polymer Clay Supplies

2 ounces of gold clay

Rolling pin

Green pigment ink pad

Craft knife

Silicone adhesive

Miscellaneous

Synthetic-bristle paintbrush

Wedge-shaped applicator sponge

Paper towels

Sea sponge

Acrylic spray sealer

*C*reate elegant, decorative planters by accenting ordinary terracotta flower pots with stamped polymer clay cutouts. The base of the pots are basecoated with acrylic paints in deep, rich colors, then stamped and sponged in gold to complement the gold rims. The individual polymer clay leaves, some of which are accented with gold paint, add textural interest.

1. Paint the base of the pot with tomato spice or eggplant acrylic paint. Let dry, then paint the rim in gold. Let dry.
2. Use a wedge sponge to ink the large leaf on the rubber stamp die with gold acrylic paint. Stamp the base by rolling the inked die in one direction over its curved surface. Re-ink the stamp after making each print.

Stamp the base of the pot by rolling the inked stamp over its curved surface.

3. Condition the clay (knead it until pliable), then roll it into a sheet approximately $^1/_8$ to $^1/_4$ inch thick. Stamp the clay with several large leaf prints, some without ink, and some with green pigment ink. (For best results, ink the stamp with a small raised ink pad.)

4. Cut around the leaf prints with a craft knife, then cure them in an oven following the manufacturer's instructions.

5. Paint both the inked and uninked polymer clay leaves with gold acrylic paint. Use a paper towel to blot the still-wet surface so that the color of the clay or the pigment ink shows through. Let dry.

6. Use the silicone adhesive to glue three leaves to the rim of the pot, alternating between gold and green, or to the base and rim of the pot in a random fashion.

7. Heighten the color of the base by applying gold paint with a sea sponge. Let dry.

8. Finish with two or three light coats of acrylic spray sealer.

Stamp the polymer clay with several prints, either in green pigment ink or without any ink at all. Trim around the prints with a craft knife, then cure in an oven.

Paint the cured leaves with gold acrylic paint, then blot the surface with a paper towel. Let dry.

Affix the leaves to the pot with silicone adhesive.

Metal-Trimmed Mirror

MATERIALS AND SUPPLIES

Project

2-inch-wide strip of pine (measure the perimeter of your mirror tile to calculate its length) OR a ready-made frame

Small square mirror tile

Square of cardboard (about 1 inch larger on all sides than the mirror tile)

Thin, flexible sheet of brass

Rubber Stamps

Sponge (A955E)

Eight-point star (A1054C)

Fleur-de-lis (A263E)

Pigment Ink Pads

Brown

Pine green

Embossing Supplies

Clear embossing ink pad

Gold embossing powder

Embossing heat tool

Miscellaneous

Paint and varnish remover and wood putty (optional, for a finished frame)

Handsaw

Medium-grit sandpaper

Tack cloth

Crackle glaze

Small flat synthetic-bristle paintbrush

Gold metallic paste

Tissue

Acrylic spray sealer

Wood glue

Tongs OR gloves (optional, for embossing the brass sheet)

Old scissors

Small metal file

Silicone adhesive

*T*his project's subtle blurred surface finish consists of several layers of stamp prints, which were then distressed by two methods: first by sanding, then by applying a crackle glaze. To make the ornaments, a thin sheet of brass was embossed with gold fleurs-de-lis, which were then cut out and glued to the corners.

The matching lidded box, shown here displaying a selection of crackers, can be made by purchasing a small wooden box, then following steps 3 through 9 of the instructions for the mirror.

1. If you're making your frame from scratch, proceed to step 2.
   If you're using a ready-made unfinished frame, go to step 3.
   If your ready-made frame is already finished, strip it with paint and varnish remover. Fill any holes or cracks with wood putty, let dry, then proceed to step 3.
2. Use the handsaw to cut the strip of pine into four pieces of equal length that correspond to the dimensions of the mirror tile. Cut the ends of each piece at a 45-degree angle.
3. Lightly sand the surface of the wood, then dust it with a tack cloth to remove any sanding dust.
4. Ink the sponge stamp with brown ink, then stamp the wood in a random fashion. Clean the stamp thoroughly, ink it with green ink, then overprint the brown prints. Let dry.

Randomly stamp the wood with sponge prints in brown and let dry. Repeat in green.

5. Ink the star stamp with green ink, then overprint the sponge prints randomly. Smudge the ink by lightly sanding the stamped surfaces, continuing until the star prints are fuzzy and vague. Let dry. Reprint the stars in green to reinforce their shape. Do not sand again. Let dry.

6. Paint the stamped surfaces with a coat of crackle glaze following the manufacturer's instructions. Let dry. Rub the gold metallic paste into the cracks with a tissue. Finish with a coat of acrylic spray sealer.

7. If you're working on a ready-made frame, go to step 8.
   If you're making your frame from scratch, use the wood glue to affix the mirror tile to the center of the cardboard square and assemble the frame. Glue the frame to the cardboard. Let dry. Proceed to step 8.

8. Ink the fleur-de-lis stamp with embossing ink, then print it on the brass sheet. Lift the stamp straight up without dragging or shifting. If you feel the stamp begin to slide, wipe off the smudged image, wash and dry the brass thoroughly, then try again. Emboss the print with gold embossing powder. While melting the powder, it's a good idea to protect your hands by wearing gloves or holding the sheet with a pair of tongs. Let cool. Repeat to make a total of four embossed prints.

9. Cut out the embossed fleur-de-lis prints with an old pair of scissors. Smooth the cut edges with a metal file. Attach an ornament to each corner of the frame with silicone adhesive. Let dry.

Overstamp the sponge prints with random green star prints, then smudge them by sanding lightly. Let dry, then reprint to clarify their shape.

Once the star prints have dried, apply crackle glaze, then let dry. Rub gold paste into the cracks with a tissue. Finish with spray sealer.

Cut out the embossed prints with an old pair of scissors, smooth cut edges with a metal file, then attach the corners of the frame with silicone adhesive.

Leather Portfolio

MATERIALS AND SUPPLIES

Project

Two 8¹/₂- × 11-inch pieces of natural-color leather

One 2-inch black horn-shaped bead

2 yards of 2mm black leather thong

Patterns

Pages 156 and 157

Rubber Stamp

Lace fern corner (A1258)

Embossing Supplies

Clear embossing ink pad

Black embossing powder

Embossing heat tool

Fabric Ink Pad

Black

Dye-Based Ink Pads

Pale aqua

Wisteria

Leather Supplies

Leather Sheen

Tanners Bond® Leathercraft Cement

³/₃₂-inch drive punch

Mallet

Miscellaneous

Stylus

Craft knife

Metal ruler

2-inch rubber brayer

Black fabric marker (optional)

New household sponge

Dusty lavender acrylic paint

Small plastic container

¹/₄- and 1-inch synthetic-bristle paintbrushes

Soft cotton cloth

*T*he perfect gift for someone who's landed their first job—or achieved a major milestone in his or her career—this elegant leather porfolio can be made to reflect the personality of the recipient by varying colors and stamp motifs.

1. Enlarge the patterns to full size. Lay the enlarged patterns over the leather pieces, then trace the following shapes with a stylus:
   - Two 8¹/₂- × 5⁷/₈-inch pieces, for the front and back covers
   - One 8¹/₂- × 2⁵/₈-inch piece, for the gusset
   - One 2¹/₂- × 5⁷/₈-inch piece, for the file pocket (inside front cover)
   - One 3¹/₄- × 2¹/₈-inch piece, for the business card holder (inside front cover)
   - Two 1¹/₂- × 5⁷/₈-inch pieces, for the pad pocket supports (inside back cover)

   To cut the leather accurately, use a craft knife and metal ruler. After cutting all the pieces, you should have two small pieces left over (one square, the other L-shaped); these scraps will serve as practice surfaces for embossing.

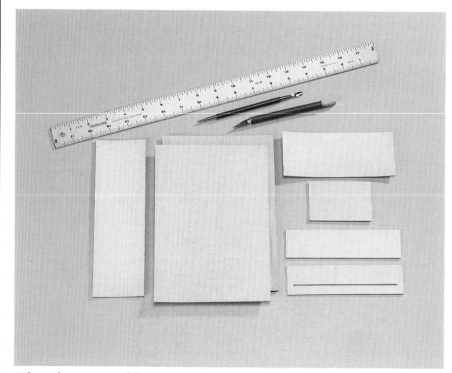

Enlarge the patterns to full size. Lay the enlarged patterns over the leather pieces, trace the shapes with a stylus, and cut the leather with a craft knife and metal ruler.

2. Use clear embossing ink and black embossing powder to emboss a lace fern print on the grain side of one of the scrap pieces. If the powder doesn't adhere well to the print, saturate the pad with a re-inker, then use a brayer to ink the stamp. Once you've successfully embossed one or two prints on the scrap pieces, repeat on the grain side of the two $8^1/_2$- × $5^7/_8$-inch pieces cut for the front and back covers. Set aside.

3. Clean the brayer thoroughly. Ink the brayer with black ink fabric, then roll it over the $8^1/_2$- × $2^5/_8$-inch piece cut for the gusset, overlapping each stroke to achieve uniform coverage. Color the edges of the gusset with a black fabric marker, or simply run them over the ink pad. Set aside. Clean the brayer for the next step.

4. Use a clean sponge to dampen the grain side of all the pieces (with the exception of the black gusset) with water; this relaxes the surface, especially of the pieces that are embossed, allowing the ink to penetrate well. Ink the brayer with pale aqua ink, then apply it randomly to the leather. Repeat with the wisteria ink. Let dry.

5. Pour a little of the lavender acrylic paint into a small container, then dilute it slightly with water. Use the $^1/_4$-inch brush to color the edges of the pieces that were brayered in the previous step. Set aside and let dry completely.

6. Rub the embossed pieces with a soft cotton cloth to remove excess dye. Spray two light coats of Leather Sheen on the grain side of all the pieces (including the gusset). Let dry.

Emboss lace fern prints on the front and back covers with clear embossing ink and black embossing powder.

7. Place the front and back cover pieces grain side up on your work surface. Adhere the gusset to the covers with Tanners Bond Leathercraft Cement, overlapping each approximately $7/8$ inch. Let dry.
8. Paint the inside of the portfolio with the slightly diluted lavender acrylic paint. Let dry.
9. Cut a $5^1/2$- × $^1/8$-inch slot in one of the pocket supports. Apply Leathercraft Cement to the edges of the undersides of the file pocket, business card holder, and pad pocket supports, then secure them in place on the inside covers. (Refer to the patterns for the position of the slot and the extent of the areas to be glued.)

Relax the surface of the leather by dampening the grain side of all the pieces (except the gusset) with water. Randomly brayer the pieces, first with pale aqua ink, then with wisteria ink. Let dry. Paint the edges with slightly diluted lavender acrylic. Let dry. Lightly spray the inked surfaces with two coats of Leather Sheen.

Assemble the cover with Leathercraft Cement, then paint the inside of the portfolio with the diluted lavender acrylic. Let dry. Glue the file pocket, business card holder, and pad pocket supports to the inside covers.

10. Using the pattern as a guide, mark the positions of the gusset holes on the spine side with the stylus. Open the portfolio, place it spine side up on your work surface, then punch the gusset holes with the drive punch and mallet.

11. Thread the horn bead onto a 24-inch length of thong. Secure the bead in the center with an overhand knot. Thread each end of the thong through the two holes in the center of the gusset so that the bead hangs approximately 3 inches from the edge of the portfolio. Secure the thong on the inside of the cover with overhand knots, trim away the excess, then place a dab of Leathercraft Cement on each knot.

12. Fold a 20-inch length of thong in half. To make a loop for the closure, tie an overhand knot approximately 1¼ inches from the fold. Thread each end of the thong through the two outer holes in the gusset. Close the portfolio to adjust the length of the closure, then secure the ends of the thong as noted in step 11.

Punch the gusset holes with the drive punch and mallet. Thread the bead onto a thong, secure it with an overhand knot, then thread the ends of the thong through the two center holes in the gusset, securing them on the inside cover. Make a loop for the closure, thread the ends through the two outer holes, close the portfolio to adjust its length, then secure the ends.

Patterns

OVERPRINTED FLORAL PLACEMAT PATTERNS
Project instructions are on pages 104–107.
Use at same size.

LEATHER PORTFOLIO CUTTING AND ASSEMBLY PATTERNS

Project instructions are on pages 150–154.

All measurements are in inches. Areas shaded in light gray indicate where glue should be applied prior to assembly.

Enlarge 153%.

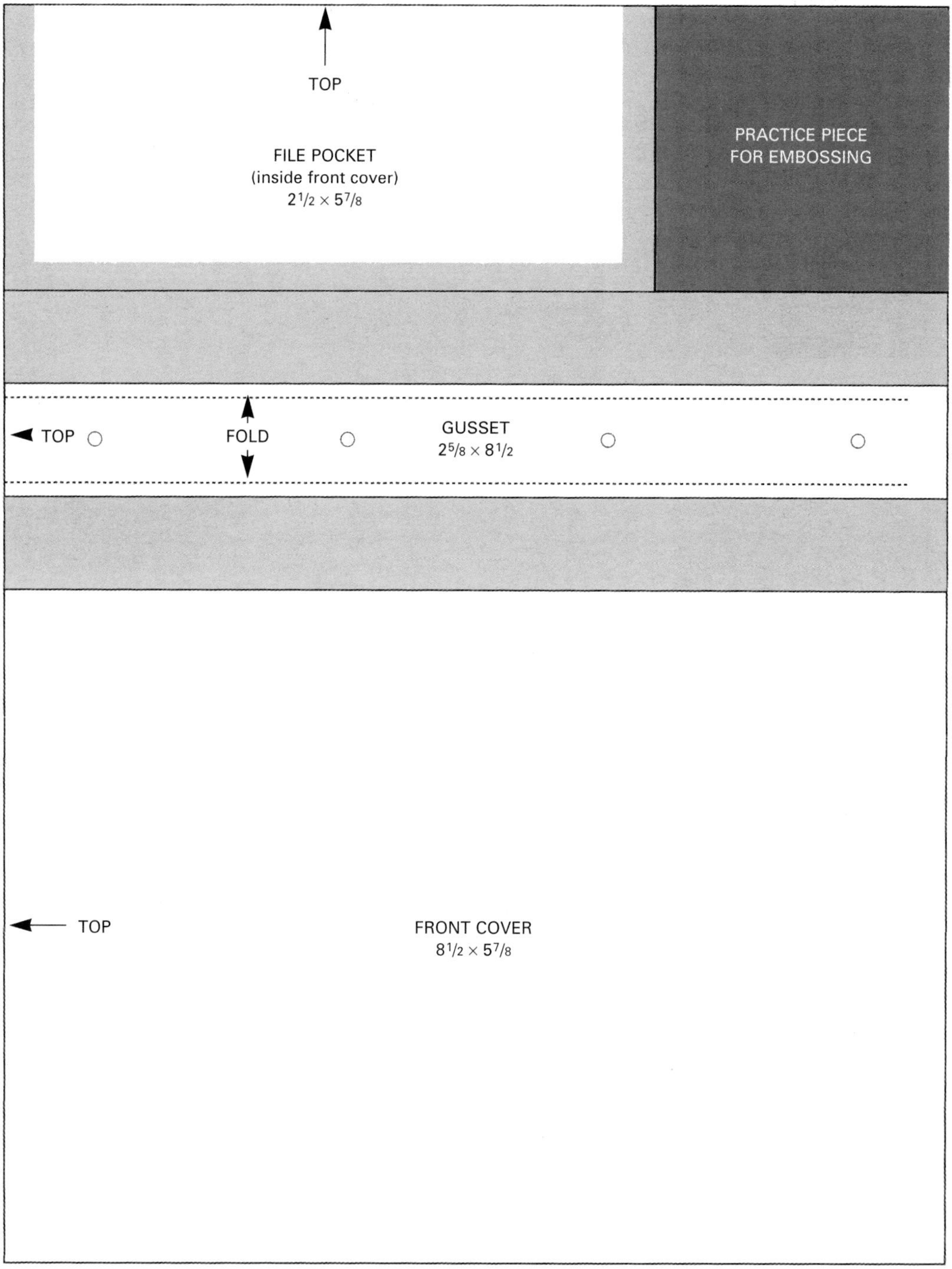

TOP

FILE POCKET
(inside front cover)
$2^1/_2 \times 5^7/_8$

PRACTICE PIECE
FOR EMBOSSING

TOP FOLD GUSSET
$2^5/_8 \times 8^1/_2$

TOP FRONT COVER
$8^1/_2 \times 5^7/_8$

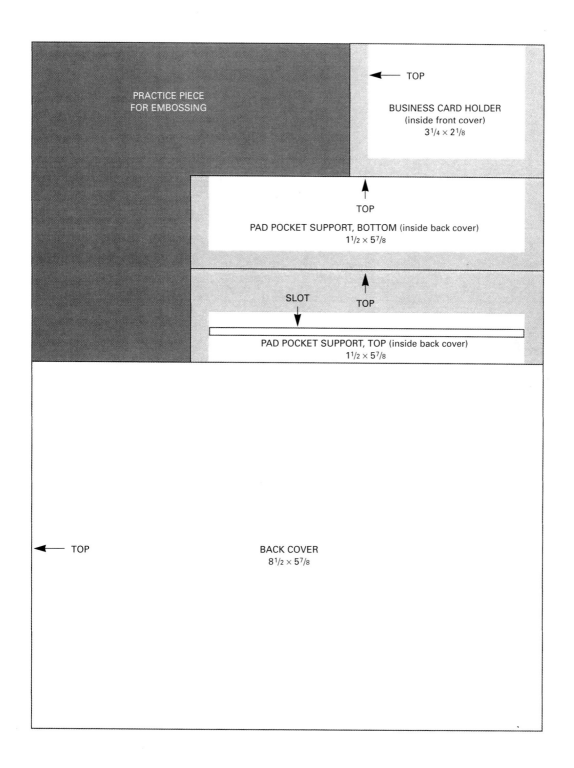

PRACTICE PIECE
FOR EMBOSSING

← TOP

BUSINESS CARD HOLDER
(inside front cover)
$3^1/4 \times 2^1/8$

↑
TOP

PAD POCKET SUPPORT, BOTTOM (inside back cover)
$1^1/2 \times 5^7/8$

SLOT   ↑ TOP
↓

PAD POCKET SUPPORT, TOP (inside back cover)
$1^1/2 \times 5^7/8$

← TOP

BACK COVER
$8^1/2 \times 5^7/8$

Source Directory

Listed at right are the manufacturers and wholesale suppliers for some of the materials used in this book. These companies generally sell their products exclusively to art supply, craft, and stamping retailers, which are a consumer's most dependable sources for stamping supplies. Your local retailers can advise you on your purchases, and if you need something they don't have in stock they will usually order it for you. If you can't find a store in your area that carries a particular item or will accept a request for an order, or if you need special technical assistance, a manufacturer will gladly direct you to the retailer nearest you that carries their products, and will try to answer any other questions you might have.

Bagworks, Inc.
3933 California Parkway
Fort Worth, Texas 96119
(817) 536-3892
Fabric blanks (pillowcases and floorcloths)

Delta Technical Coatings
2550 Pellissier Place
Whittier, California 90601
(800) 423-4135
Acrylic and ceramic paints and antiquing medium

The Leather Factory
3847 East Loop 820 South
Fort Worth, Texas 76119
(800) 433-3201
Leather and suede yardage

Marvy/Uchida
3535 Del Amo Boulevard
Torrance, California 90503
(310) 793-2200
Brush markers, embossing heat tools, and Liquid Appliqué™

Mixed Nuts
219 Rayon Drive
Old Hickory, Tennessee 37138
(615) 847-8399
Corrugated cardboard child's chair (page 58)

Polyform Products Co.
1904 Estes Avenue
Elk Grove Village, Illinois 60007
(847) 427-0020
Polymer clay

Rubber Stampede
P.O. Box 246
Berkeley, California 94701
(800) NEAT-FUN (632-8386)
Supplier for all the rubber and foam stamp images and inks, stamp pads, and stamping paints featured in this book. Corresponding item numbers are cited in the materials list for each project.

Rupert, Gibbon & Spider, Inc.
P.O. Box 425
Healdsburg, California 95448
(800) 442-0455
Pearl Ex Powdered Pigments

The Speedball Art Products Co.
P.O. Box 5157
Satesville, North Carolina 28687
Printing blocks, linoleum, brayers, and carving tools

Suze Weinberg
39 Old Bridge Road
Howell, New Jersey 07731
(732) 364-3136
Suze Weinberg's Ultra Thick Embossing Enamel

Tsukineko
15411 N.E. 95th Street
Redmond, Washington 98052
(206) 883-7733
Embossing pens

USArtQuest, Inc.
P.O. Box 88
Chelsea, Michigan 48118
(313) 475-7622
Perfect Paper Adhesive™

Victoria Paper Company
80-28 Springfield Boulevard
Hollis Hills, New York 11427-1232
(718) 740-0990
Handmade art papers

Walnut Hollow
Route 2
Dodgeville, Wisconsin 53533
(608) 935-2341
Wood blanks (frames, boxes, trays, and plates)

Index